Group
Participation

SAGE HUMAN SERVICES GUIDES

A series of books edited by ARMAND LAUFFER and CHARLES D. GARVIN. Published in cooperation with the University of Michigan School of Social Work and other organizations.

Group
Participation

Techniques for
Leaders and Members

Second Edition

Harvey J. Bertcher

SHSG SAGE HUMAN
SERVICES GUIDE 10

*Published in cooperation with the University
of Michigan School of Social Work*

SAGE Publications
International Educational and Professional Publisher
Thousand Oaks   London   New Delhi

For information address:

 SAGE Publications, Inc.
2455 Teller Road
Thousand Oaks, California 91320
E-mail: order@sagepub.com

SAGE Publications Ltd.
6 Bonhill Street
London EC2A 4PU
United Kingdom

SAGE Publications India Pvt. Ltd.
M-32 Market
Greater Kailash I
New Delhi 110 048 India

Printed in the United States of America

Library of Congress Cataloging-in-Publication Data

Bertcher, Harvey J.
   Group participation: techniques for leaders and members / Harvey J.
Bertcher. —2nd ed.
     p. cm.—(Sage human services guide: v. 10)
   Includes bibliographical references and indexes.
   ISBN 0-8039-5213-9 (cl.)—ISBN 0-8039-5214-7 (pbk.)
   1. Small groups. 2. Social groups. 3. Social participation.
4. Leadership. I. University of Michigan. School of Social Work.
II. Title. III. Series.
HM133.B483 1994
649'.1—dc20
                                   94-31224

99 00 01 02 03 9 8 7 6 5

Sage Production Editor: Diane S. Foster

CONTENTS

For Jesse Gordon, who made this book possible;
Tim Sampson, who asked me to write it;

Ruby Pernell
Hank Linville
Dorothea Spellmann
Irv Kaplan
Elwood Saunders
Helen Northen

all of whom tried to teach me how
to think about and work with groups;
and Gloria, Quincey and Corey—
my own "effective" and affective group

PREFACE

After 10 printings of this book, we decided it was time for an update. To assist me in doing this, Sage solicited opinions from three faculty members from around the country who had made use of the text, and copies of their suggestions were sent to me. In addition, one of the three, a professor of sociology, had his or her students write their suggestions. All of these comments proved invaluable, for they provided my first view of readers who were not also students in my own classes. All in all, the comments were constructive; in some cases, surprising; in some cases, negative; and in all cases, useful. I have tried to keep them in mind, along with some of my own ideas for improvement, as I worked on this second edition.

The editors for this series, Armand Lauffer and Charles Garvin (who happen, fortunately for me, also to be colleagues here at the University of Michigan School of Social Work) had agreed that a weak point of the book was its attempt to serve as the basis for an innovation in educational practice—namely, a self-instructional classroom *sans professeur*. Therefore, all references to making the book serve in this way were to be omitted. Nevertheless, our sociology professor made it clear that was exactly what made the book useful for her or his purposes. The book (I was informed) is used as a supplemental text in a larger course on sociology, in which one part of the course involves having the students learn small group theory by participating in a small group that focuses around the "techniques" presented herein. Remove *that* aspect of the book, and it would no longer be useful. The current version does not highlight the role of the Convener (a rotating position that allows group members to take turns running the group so as to experience formal group leadership) in the way that the first edition did, but it retains the small group exercises. It still allows a group to participate in discussions about an array of group processes and issues, then review itself for further insights and skill development.

The introductory chapter on the nature of the small group has been updated and enlarged, and an epilogue has been added to begin the necessary task of relating the leadership techniques to the various types of groups in which they are to be used. The write-ups themselves have been revised, and three new sections have been added to each chapter. The first one is used to raise a diverse set of issues about group leadership (one issue for each technique). The second is used to alert the group to things it should do to prepare for the next session. The third adds an important area that had been missing in the first edition: the issues of oppression and empowerment for population groups that have had extensive experience with prejudice and discrimination. Finally, the bibliographies at the end of each chapter have been updated.

The feedback from the three faculty—two of whom teach social work courses—helped me to understand that this book may be used best as a supplemental, rather than as a main, text for teaching purposes. In that role, its size, design, and comparatively low cost in today's market, apparently make it useful for a variety of purposes. What more can an author hope for?

I would like to express my appreciation for the secretarial support of Kathleen Cornell, Barbara Hochrein, Roxanne Loy, and Marcie McKinley. Further, I want to thank Armand Lauffer and Charles Garvin for the opportunity to revisit the written premises in an attempt to make them more usable.

HARVEY J. BERTCHER

PREFACE TO THE FIRST EDITION

Anyone working in a human service organization is likely to be involved with groups—perhaps as an inservice trainer orienting a new group of staff members, a citizen board member working out a new policy, a chair of a staff committee, a co-leader of a treatment group, or part of a staff team in a problem-solving meeting—the list is endless. In every one of these groups, there are some basic techniques that, if used correctly, can help make the group successful: successful as regards both goal achievement and participant satisfaction. This book originally was designed to provide instruction in these basic techniques based on the assumption that everyone who participates in a group, whether formally designated as "Leader" (with a capital "L") or as "member," has the responsibility and the ability to help the group succeed. Accordingly, this book was meant to be useful to Leaders (e.g., group workers, presidents, chairpersons, discussion leaders, classroom teachers, child care workers, unit supervisors, club leaders, group therapists) as well as members (e.g., constituents, colleagues, clients, patients, students) because they could be viewed as participants in a group.

Once published, however, the first edition of this book was discovered by persons who wanted to teach about theory and process in small groups—for example, in a sociology course. These instructors wanted to include an actual small group experience for their students as part of the instructional process, and they found that this book provided the basis for the kind of "hands-on" experience they wanted their students to have. So although the book initially was intended for potential leaders and members, its second major audience has turned out to be

ix

students of small group theory who want to learn about groups through participation in one.

You may be interested to know how this book came to be written, tested, and revised to its current form. It began as a project on group leadership techniques by Manpower Science Services, Inc., a small nonprofit corporation established in 1968 to make social science knowledge more useful in helping the unemployed and underemployed. The development work that was involved in creating the *Techniques of Group Leadership Handbook* and associated teaching materials was supported by the Manpower Administration, U.S. Department of Labor, under Contract No. 82-24-70-23. Because contractors performing such work under government sponsorship are encouraged to express their own judgment freely, the *Handbook* had no connection with the department's official opinion or policy.

Interest in a training package on group leadership techniques came from the Division of Utilization of the Manpower Administration. Its support was for a larger project that would explore the problems attendant to the utilization of social science research in the development of innovations in service delivery, as well as in the problems attendant to diffusion and use of the innovations. The project on group leadership was but one of a series of four,[1] each relating to different steps in the entire process of innovation diffusion and utilization.

I was project director for the group leadership effort, and as such, took major responsibility for writing several drafts of the *Handbook*. A great many people, however, worked to produce the instructional package. The process of development went something like this: An initial version of the package was tried out informally in one human resources agency whose staff participated with Manpower Science Services in packaging the instructions into a handbook, film, and convener's manual. The first package was then tried out in five human resources agencies around the country. Follow-up with participants in these five agencies included questionnaires, personal interviews, and conferences. On the basis of that experience, the materials were further revised. That revision was further edited by human resources agency workers before being put into a final form. The package was then made available to human resources agencies around the country.

As a faculty member of the University of Michigan's School of Social Work, I was able to introduce the package into our curriculum as a special studies self-managed course for small groups of students who took it on a pass/fail basis. It was my observation that the content and the teaching approach were unique and had definite values for graduate students. I also discovered, however, that several aspects of the package needed to be improved or discarded if the materials were to be optimally useful to our students, as well as for the many human service organizations and other graduate and undergraduate programs that came to use it.

In the first edition, the film was dropped, to be replaced with a number of vignettes in script form (readers referred to them as "skits") depicting a wide variety of small group situations. Material from a separate Convener's Manual was incorporated into the book. Some practice exercises that did not work were dropped, while some new and it is hoped more fruitful exercises were added.

In the first edition the chapter on group creation was dropped, because a much richer version of that chapter's contents was written as a programmed instruction book and published separately (see Bertcher & Maple, 1977). The write-ups of each technique were reviewed for greater clarity of language and consistency with research findings. Originally, literature reviews covering research relevant to each technique were included in the *Handbook,* but page limitations of the **Sage Human Services Guides** series forced me to drop these reviews. In their place, suggested readings have been cited at the end of each chapter so that the interested reader can study the major sources on which each chapter is based. Although I am a social worker and the content reflects this bias to some degree, I have tried to write for a wide variety of potential audiences, many of whom work in or with groups that do not meet to provide social work services to clients (see, for example, The Parent Teacher Organization committee script for the chapter on Rewarding, the staff meeting script for Focusing and the Citizens Advisory Committee script for Mediating: each of these falls in the general category of "task groups").

Obviously, there were many people in the human resources field and other human service organizations who contributed to the creation of the original set of materials, and credit cannot be given to all. The bulk of the research, designing, and writing on the Labor Department's version of the *Handbook* were done by the following Manpower Science Services staff, in addition to myself: Jesse Gordon, Ph.D. (also Professor of Psychology and Social Work, University of Michigan); Steven Aigner, Ph.D.; Steven Fabricant, M.B.A.; Michael Hayes, Ph.D.; Pam Kladzyk, B.F.A.; Robert Kozma, Ph.D.; Melvyn Lawson, M.S.W.; Jerome Munsey, M.S.W.; Joni Rosenwach, B.A.; William Shade, M.S.W.; and Annette Weiss, M.Ed.

Staff members of human resources agencies who served as conveners during field tests and who devoted untold hours to editing drafts, critiquing, advising, and suggesting improvements were: Alexandra Lucky, Joe Norris, Marion Lyon (all from the Michigan Employment

Security Commission); Elizabeth Pamplin and Ronald Barkett (from the Florida Department of Commerce); and Robert Guy and James Schatz (from the Colorado Employment Commission).

Vital support for the project was provided by Howard Rosen, Director, Office of Research and Development, U.S. Department of Labor; and Judah Drob, Chief, Division of Utilization, Office of Employment and Training Research, U.S. Department of Labor.

The editorial comments of Armand Lauffer have been extremely helpful in giving this package a more generic quality, so that it could be useful to the full range of people who work in human service organizations. But the final responsibility rests with me, and I trust you will not think too unkindly of the results.

HARVEY BERTCHER

NOTE

1. The other three projects each resulted in a product: *Role Modeling and Role Playing* (a manual), 1969; *Simulation and Imitation* (a set of audio cassette tapes and a workbook), 1971; and *Local Office Decision Making and Implementation* (a manual for a self-instructional workshop), 1976. All were produced by Manpower Science Services, Inc. (an organization that is no longer in existence).

Chapter 1

INTRODUCTION
The Effective Group

People sometimes skip or skim introductions. Don't. Read this one carefully. It will tell you what to expect from this experience and how to make it work for you. It also contains a discussion of the term *group* that is basic to understanding the chapters that follow.

You are about to read a book from which you can learn how to employ techniques that are useful when participating in groups as either a leader or a member. Much of what is in this book should be familiar: You have probably been in groups in which the leader, teacher, chairperson, or other member used similar techniques. Perhaps you have used them yourself in groups or in one-on-one interviews.

What may appear different at first is seeing these techniques spelled out in such a detailed way: concise descriptions of each technique; detailed discussions of when, how, and why to use them; related issues of oppression and empowerment; concrete examples in scripted vignettes; exercises designed to provide practice; some discussion of a pertinent issue; and references to relevant behavioral science literature. The purpose of assembling the information this way is to give you a knowledge base of the techniques for you to use when you participate in a group, either as its formal leader or as a member.

Upon completion of this book, you should be able to make appropriate and confident use of these techniques when occupying the position of leader or member of a group. Regardless of your position, you will be able to help the group achieve its goals, as well as help individual members achieve their personal goals.

This introductory chapter includes a discussion of the term *group*—a much misunderstood and misused word—and its relationship to group participation techniques.

WHAT IS MEANT BY THE TERM *GROUP?*

Before reading the discussion that follows, write your definition of *group* in the space below without reference to any source other than your own thoughts. (Assume that you are defining *group* in relation to people.) Write the most thorough definition you can: You will be comparing it with mine. Then write the names of (or descriptive terms for) three groups to which you now belong.

I would define the word *group* as

_____

_____

Three groups I belong to now are

1. _____

2. _____

3. _____

Now rate the degree to which you think these three groups are successful and why you think so. This should provide you with a way of making the discussion that follows relevant to your personal experience.

I would rate the success of each group as

1. _____ Very successful   _____ Fairly successful
   _____ Not too successful   _____ Not successful at all

2. _____ Very successful   _____ Fairly successful
   _____ Not too successful   _____ Not successful at all

3. _____ Very successful   _____ Fairly successful
   _____ Not too successful   _____ Not successful at all

WRITING IN THE BOOK

From time to time, you will be asked to write answers in the book to questions I want you to think about. I hope that this form of active response will facilitate what you learn from this book. Obviously, if this book is not your personal copy, you should write your answers in a notebook, not on the pages of the book. But you should *write* your answers—don't just think about them. Writing is a way of requiring you to commit to something and, in this case, should prove useful to you.

Here is my definition of *group,*[1] based in part on Shaw's (1976) review of several definitions:

A group is a dynamic social entity composed of two or more individuals. These individuals interact interdependently to achieve one or more common goals for the group or similar individual goals that each member believes can best be achieved through group participation. As a result of this participation, each member influences and is influenced by every other member to some degree. Over time, statuses and roles develop for members, while norms and values that regulate behavior of consequence to the group are accepted by members.

One thing that makes this definition so interesting pertains to the phrase, "over time". Some groups that meet for a long period of time are "closed," meaning the same individuals who attend the first meeting continue to comprise the group—with no change—until it terminates (e.g., an undergraduate course). Other groups are "open," meaning membership changes from meeting to meeting (Galinsky & Schopler, 1989). The most extreme example of an open meeting is the single-session group that meets once and never again (see, for example, Block, 1985). Open-ended groups can be described in terms of how often individual members enter and leave the group and how long each remains in the group once he or she has joined it. In social work, an example of a single-session group (in which all members are new each time the group meets, but the same social worker conducts each new group) is an orientation group for patients and their family members who meet at the time the patient enters the hospital for diagnosis and treatment of cancer. Less frequent, but predictable, change in membership can be seen in therapeutic camps where campers come for varying, but fixed, periods of stay. Frequent, but not extensive, change can be seen in inpatient groups in drug rehabilitation centers. Less frequent and less extensive change can be seen in psychotherapy groups in which membership change can occur, but only after many months.

The "closed or open" nature of a group, and the *degree* to which it is "open" of necessity, affects all aspects of group structure and process and should be kept in mind throughout the reading of this book. For example, the formal leader of the single-session group, which operates with a very limited time frame, will, by necessity, need to be very active in all aspects of the group's operations, from the clarity of expectations the leader must impart to potential members (about the goals and nature of the group) to the limitations involved in the group's contract. The formal leader (or "therapist") of a psychotherapy group, however, can be much more relaxed about having a contract negotiated early in the first meeting, and the leader can purposely adopt a low visibility approach to leadership in the expectation that group members will gradually become active in the performance of leadership functions.

How does this discussion compare to your definition of the term *group?* How well do the three groups you listed fit *this* definition? Having a clear working definition of *group* is important because you often find yourself involved with a collection of people who are either an "underdeveloped" or an "unsuccessful" group; that is, members have not dealt effectively with some of the elements of the group specified by the above definition—elements that are essential to group development. Also, the group is not working with regard to the purpose for which it was created.

A key question may therefore be, When is a group *not* a group? That is, When does a collection of individuals lack clarity about—or have insufficient amounts of—some of the elements listed in the definition that are essential to becoming a *successful* group? Once we recognize that every collection of individuals is not necessarily a successful group, we can begin to think about using techniques of group participation to help the members *become* a successful group.

WHEN IS A GROUP *NOT* A GROUP?

Consider the case of a person, A, who is looking up at the sky and is approached, independently, by two other persons, B and C, who also begin looking in the same direction. . . . No group exists, despite the fact that B and C (may) have been influenced by A (to look at the sky) because A has not been influenced by B and C. These three persons become a group if they enter into a discussion (interaction) concerning the object of their attention. An aggregate of individuals is a group only if interaction occurs. (Shaw, 1976, p. 11)

More accurately, this collection of three individuals is a very particular kind of pre-group circumstance; for although they do interact simply in the sense of being *aware* of one another, their common goal may be to share the pleasure of sky-gazing, after which they go their separate ways.

Thus their "group" as a social entity has no further existence. I assume that readers of this book are interested in groups that have a somewhat longer life span and more significant goals, such as staff-work units, committees, classes, treatment groups, policy-making boards, clubs, and so forth. Accordingly, the three sky watchers referred to above have the *potential* of becoming the kind of successful group with which this book is concerned, but they are not a "group" as the term is used in this book.

The above discussion is not meant to imply that a group exists simply because the same people meet together over a period of time. For example,

a community mental health program functioned through the activities of six highly autonomous units, each located in a different part of the city. The agency's director would periodically call meetings of the individuals who supervised a unit. When the six supervisors met with the director, their attitude was one of, "Let's get this over with as soon as possible so that we can get back to work." The interaction that took place was polite but forced; most communication went from the director to the supervisors, with almost no communication *among* the supervisors. The reason for this situation was clear. The six units did not rely on one another; that is, they were not interdependent and met only to satisfy the Director's need to be in touch with each supervisor without having to go to six different locations. It was not that they could not have *become* a group; they simply had no reason for becoming one, because they shared no common tasks and no common goals. Accordingly, they had no need to develop the ways of working together that are characteristic of a successful group.

WHAT MAKES A GROUP SUCCESSFUL?

FIRST: COMMON GOAL(S)

A successful group is one that fits my definition of "group" in a positive sense; that is, it comprises two or more individuals who interact over time to achieve one or more group (i.e., common) goals or to achieve individual goals that are valued by each member who believes that *this* group can help him or her achieve them. Further, they interact in such a way that each must be dependent on the other to some degree as they try to achieve either group or individual goals, and each feels that they have been able to influence the others to some degree. In a successful group—one that has *become* successful—the statuses and roles of each member and the values and norms that guide the behavior of the members are well known and generally accepted.

Think of the three groups to which you said you currently belong. How well do they fit this definition of a successful group? Are there perhaps other factors that make them more or less successful? For example, take the common goal(s) question:

Assume that Tom, Dick, and Harry each wants to marry Jane. Is that a common goal? Assuming that each communicates to the others his feelings toward Jane, are they a group? Hardly. They have the same individual goal but not a **common** goal; that is, each has a desired goal in mind for himself but interdependent interaction is not likely to achieve the individual goal of each to marry Jane (at least, not in our monogamous society). It is possible that if Sam, Pete, and John happen along and are also interested in Jane, Tom, Dick, and Harry might temporarily become a group in order to drive off the interlopers. But once this is accomplished, this group would fall apart because the individual motive of each precludes a common effort; that is, each of them does *not* believe that working together could help them achieve their individual goal.

Common goal refers to some state or condition that the majority of the members wish to see occur for their group. A common goal of a committee might be to achieve consensus on the wording of a report that it has been asked to prepare, and then to get copies of the report to the right people in time for a particular meeting. What is the common goal of a classroom? That is trickier, because some classes never become successful groups anymore than Tom, Dick, and Harry did. Each student pursues (hopefully) knowledge for his or her own use and (certainly) for a passing grade in the course. Often the student can achieve both knowledge and a passing grade *without* interdependent interaction. (Anyone who has ever sat through a lecture class with 500 other students can attest to the accuracy of this statement!) And if grading is highly competitive, they are even less likely to become a group. What often happens in classes is that small numbers of students band together informally for mutual support, such as swapping notes, studying together, and so on. An entire class *can* become a successful group, however, if, for example, they work together to complete a class project. A tremendous amount of individual learning can still take place in a class that does *not* become a successful group as a total class.

A work unit in a public welfare department may get the job done— that is, service to individual clients—without ever becoming an effective task group. In fact, many work units are very successful in terms of providing *informal social support* to one another in the form of friendship, interest in one another's personal life, and so on. They may never develop as successful task groups, however, because they lack common tasks and the common goal to successfully complete these tasks. This is unfortunate because groups are often superior to individuals when complex problem solving is needed (Forsyth, 1990, pp. 277-280). For example:

An employment and training unit in a public welfare agency found itself faced with an apparently insurmountable problem: finding jobs for welfare recipients in the inner city at a time of extremely high unemployment. Faced with this situation, they did the best they could with their individual case loads and were generally unsuccessful. It never occurred to them to work together as a group to determine how other employment programs in other cities had dealt with the same problem. Had they done so, they would have discovered several approaches that had a significantly higher success rate than theirs. But they were not a task group and never thought of themselves in this way. They rarely held staff meetings. When they met, it was to be informed of new policies and procedures, not to engage in group problem solving. As a result, they had no group (task) goals and continued to experience a sense of failure on their jobs.

The common goal of a treatment group may be to create an island of mutual support in which members help each other work on their individual problems so that each can return to his or her own environment with a greater capacity to deal with problems in that environment. In some cases, however, that may prove to be an insufficient goal.

Fairweather (1980), for example, reported on a group-based treatment approach to the psychiatric problems of hospitalized veterans. Although effective in helping them prepare for discharge as individuals (an individual goal), the men were not able to maintain their improvement when they returned individually to the community. Accordingly, the goal of the group was changed to provide mutual support for one another during the period following hospitalization, and the entire treatment group moved from the hospital into a community-based half-way house *together.* The results were far more gratifying in relation to the achievement of one of the group's common goals, which was: Members should not have to return to the hospital for further treatment once they have been discharged.

These examples suggest that the term *group goal* does *not* refer to a composite of individual goals (as with Tom, Dick, and Harry) unless a particular end state or condition is desired by a majority of the group's members, *and* the achievement of this end state or condition could be satisfying to a majority of the members. As Shaw (1976) notes, however:

It is important to recognize that individual goals that are not a part of the group goal do not cease to influence an individual's behavior just because he becomes a member and accepts the goal or goals of that group. The group member may be trying to achieve only individual goals, only group goals, or both individual and group goals when he engages in a particular set of activities. Usually he is attempting to achieve both, simultaneously. The relative strength of individual and group goals, and the degree to which both can be achieved by the same activities, help to determine how (successful) the group will be in achieving its goal. (Shaw, p. 298)

Finally, for a desired end state or condition to be the goal of a successful group, members must recognize that they cannot achieve it unless they can learn to depend on one another, that is, be interdependent in order to achieve the goal.

INTERDEPENDENCE IN THE SUCCESSFUL GROUP

Consider the example of three boys who join forces to create a lemonade stand. One joins the group because it gives him an opportunity to use his new set of woodworking tools to construct the stand. The second wants to make enough money to buy a new baseball glove. The third likes to be with the first two boys. Although their individual motivations differ, their common goal is to make the lemonade stand operational. To do this, the boys must depend on one another's special interests and expertise.

The more that members rely on one another for the achievement of the goals associated with a particular group, the more successful the group can become, as long as each member performs acceptably well in relation to the expectations of the other members. Earlier you listed three groups to which you now belong: In what ways and to what degree are the members interdependent? Does each member provide (as in the example of the lemonade stand) some special expertise or other resource without which the group's goals could not be achieved? Or perhaps, as in a card game, each member is performing in a similar fashion, but the group's activity could not proceed without particular kinds of interactions among its members. Or perhaps the members of your groups are supporting each other in a common defense against some environmental factor. Given an agreed-upon set of goals, a collection of individuals will not become a successful group unless its members can learn to function interdependently and are willing to do so.

If a group is to be successful, two kinds of interdependent behaviors must be performed by members: *task* behaviors—those related to goal achievement—and *socioemotional* behaviors—related to maintaining harmonious relations among members while they are working to achieve goals. Bales and Strodbeck (1951) list the following as task behaviors:

- Giving suggestions or direction or implying autonomy for others
- Giving opinions, evaluation, or analysis or expressing feelings or wishes
- Giving orientation or information or repeating or confirming
- Asking for orientation or information or repeating or confirming
- Asking for opinion, evaluation, or analysis or expressing feeling
- Asking for suggestions, direction, or possible ways to act

They list the following as positive socioemotional behaviors:

- Showing solidarity, raising the status of others, giving help, rewarding
- Showing tension release, joking, laughing, showing satisfaction
- Agreeing, showing passive acceptance, or understanding, concurring, complying

Negative[2] socioemotional behaviors include:

- Disagreeing, showing passive rejection, formality, and withholding help
- Showing tension, asking for help, withdrawing out of field
- Showing antagonism, deflating other's status, defending or asserting self

Put more simply, if members of a group devote all of their interaction to goal achievement and fail to pay attention to the conflicts, hurt feelings, and tensions that are a natural part of problem solving, sooner or later some members will find the group unattractive and leave or cease active participation. On the other hand, a group that devotes *all* of its energies to keeping members happy by avoiding internal conflict is unlikely to achieve its goals—goals that are important to its members. Failure to achieve these goals could cause members to view the group as unsuccessful and to leave or cease constructive participation. In short, if the group is to be successful, members need to be able to rely on one another, that is, become interdependent for the performance of *both* task and socioemotional behaviors.

If members are to become successfully interdependent, they have to be able to predict how the others in the group are likely to behave; that is, they have to have fairly accurate role expectations for one another.

STATUS AND ROLE IN THE SUCCESSFUL GROUP

Human beings are curious animals: We want to know why or how something happens, because the answers to these questions provide the ability to predict events in our environment and thus, we hope, to control them. This is understandable when one recognizes how poorly humans are equipped to survive in their environment in terms of physical prowess and equipment. The bird, turtle, ant, or coyote all are better endowed to survive physically and instinctively than are humans. Accordingly, humans in general, and scientists and explorers in particular, struggle to find the answers to the secrets of life, so that we can survive the perils involved in existence.

In social life, too, humans want very much to be able to predict how others will behave, and how to behave toward others, so as to maximize the rewards we receive from others, while minimizing our costs. As members of a group come to know one another, this hunger to predict is played out in the development of statuses and roles. *Status* refers to the position one occupies in a social entity: In a group it is most often associated with the status of one person over another, resulting in the ability of one person to influence the behavior of others. *Role* refers to the set of behaviors that someone in a particular status is expected to perform. When a chairperson raps a gavel and calls a meeting to order, we react favorably because the chair is performing the way we expect a chair to behave. But if the chair calls a meeting for 8:00 p.m. and everyone is present at the appointed time, but at 8:20 the chair is still chatting informally with someone at the back of the room, we get annoyed and may even attempt to pressure the chair to perform according to our expectations by asking sarcastically if her or his watch is still running.

Historically, people have tended to look to persons who occupy formal leadership positions (i.e., a supervisor, chairperson, teacher, social worker, or club leader) to assume the major responsibility for performing leadership acts. Over time, however, leadership has been reconceptualized. "Leadership is viewed as the performance of those acts that help the group to achieve its preferred outcome" (Cartwright & Zander, 1968, p. 304). In other words, anyone who asks that late-starting chairperson to start the meeting is performing what turns out to be a leadership act *if* the question prompts the chair to start the meeting.[3] This notion is central to the purpose of the book and explains my reason for stressing the use of these techniques by group participants, whether they are in formal leadership positions or not. For it is my assertion, supported by a considerable body of research, that a successful group is one in which leadership functions are shared by all members to some degree.[4] There is no rule, for example, that says only the leader can ask the quiet member to express an opinion: Any member can do it. This is true for every technique covered in the book. One should aspire to learn and use these techniques in any group, whether one does or does not have formal responsibility for running the group.[5] Of course, there are questions of timing—that is, when to use a technique—and this is covered in the discussion of each technique. In some groups, too, the members will expect the formal leader to perform leadership acts if no one else does. For example:

> The Parent Teachers Organization Board was suffering because the president did not know how to conduct a meeting. As a result, discussions wandered every which way, decisions were left dangling, and meetings that should have taken no more than 2½ hours tapered off to a weak and often unsatisfactory conclusion after 4 hours of inaction. When the president left the community, the vice president took over. The group told him they wanted to start at 7:30 p.m. and be out by 10:00. If they wandered or delayed making a decision, he was to keep them on track. Given this understanding on everyone's part, the group began to function well. Occasionally, the new president had to crack the whip, but it was always done with good humor and received in the same spirit. Meetings that had been boring and ineffective became interesting and productive. And, although it was the president who ultimately called "time" on some discussions, the members of the board now began to call one another when they got off target or delayed facing a tough decision. In short, it had become a successful group in part because roles had been clarified and members had come to see that they, too, had a responsibility to help the group end on time.

As members become increasingly clear about what to expect from one another, and about what is expected of them in helping the group to achieve its goals (assuming these expectations are acceptable to them), the group is more likely to become successful.

CREATING A SUCCESSFUL GROUP

Imagine a basketball team at a major university. Here is a group with a single, overriding goal: to win all of its games, including the championship of the athletic conference to which the school belongs. The members of the team fully recognize how essential it is to be interdependent, and all of their practice sessions are devoted to learning their respective roles so that individual performances can be well-coordinated. All of the team members, from the star center to the reserve bench warmers, share the same values

about winning, team play, and school spirit. In short, there is every reason
to believe that if they are well-coached and possess the necessary skills,
they will become a successful group.

The one element that this brief description has omitted, however, is
how individuals get to be members of the team. Surely, in this day of
high-priced intercollegiate athletics and the early departure of coaches
with losing records, no coach worth his or her salt can afford to allow
team membership to be determined by whoever happens to show up for
the first day of tryouts. In fact, extensive recruiting and seductive
athletic scholarships are the rule of the day. Coaches know that one step
in creating a successful team (group) is to locate and secure those
individuals who have demonstrated (usually by their performance on a
high school team) their ability to meet the membership criteria of a
winning team.

The way in which individuals become group members has a lot to do
with the success of a group. Reflect on the meaning of *group membership* in the following situations:

> Young men or women in a state training school cottage who must live together
>   because a juvenile court judge sent them there—particularly when they
>   believe that the judge is more likely to let them remain in the commu-
>   nity on probation if they are white and more likely to send them to a
>   training school if they are black
> Young men or women who have volunteered to play basketball at a college
>   whose basketball teams consistently lose
> New employees of a public welfare agency who are assigned to an existing
>   work unit in which all 10 members of the unit share a common
>   supervisor

In each situation, the way in which members *become* members affects
their attitude toward the group and toward themselves as members of
that group. If members are pleased to have been invited to join, or see
the acquisition of membership in a particular group as a triumph, they
are more likely to want to contribute to group success. Obviously, a
group's good reputation enhances the value of membership in it, but
membership on a losing basketball team need not be aversive if new
members are warmly received by the group and if they are assured that,
although winning is prized, the fun of playing and the camaraderie of
team play are also important.

Given the wide variety of groups in which group participation techniques could be used to increase a group's success, the following

generalizations about the relationship of membership to group success can be made:

1. Regardless of the way in which an individual becomes a member, a group is more likely to be successful if the new member feels that he or she is warmly received as a new member.

2. Marginal members—members who are denied, in some way, full access to the rights and responsibilities of group membership—are likely to be indifferent to or hostile toward the group. The successful group makes a clear distinction between its members and nonmembers by defining what makes someone a full-fledged member.

3. A group that wishes to be successful would benefit from involving senior members in the recruitment and selection of new member(s) as much as possible. This often requires that senior members clarify membership criteria before recruiting individuals to join the group. Because new members would probably be accepted on the basis of the potential they demonstrate for helping the group achieve its goals, clarification of membership criterion should lead to clarification of group goals. As previously indicated, clarity and widespread acceptance of group goals are essential if a group is to be successful.

OPPRESSION AND EMPOWERMENT

Unfortunately, today's world is one in which numerous populations experience oppression and disempowerment. Sadly, the list is long and includes people identified by class, race, ethnicity, culture, gender, sexual orientation, age, religion, mental and physical disability, national origin, former clienthood, and others. Most groups with which social workers work have members of at least one of these population groups. In one sense, the techniques presented in this book have no particular identity with any of these populations and can be used to benefit any group member, regardless of his or her population membership. But people who use these techniques do not work in an environmental vacuum. In choosing goals and/or operating procedures for a particular group, attention should be given to the ways in which the group can help its members increase their level of consciousness regarding the oppressive conditions in their lives. In addition, the group can empower its members to defeat the social oppression they face.

Because I feel very strongly that these techniques be used to combat oppression and enhance empowerment, among other things, on both an individual and group level, I have included a section called "Oppression and Empowerment" in each chapter, starting in Chapter 2.

POSTSCRIPT

Discussion of the successful group is incomplete without a nod in the direction of the group's composition and size. In *Creating Groups* (Bertcher & Maple, 1977), we noted that the composition of a group can have a powerful impact on its success. Essentially, we stated that members could be described in terms of two types of attributes: *descriptive* (i.e., categories of individuals who are similar in some respect, such as gender, age, ethnicity) and *behavioral*, (i.e., a tendency to act in some predictable way, such as "talkative," "domineering," "humorous," "task-focused"). Our research suggested that groups generally are more successful when members are *homogeneous* with regard to critical descriptive attributes that pertain to a group's goals and *heterogeneous* with regard to critical behavioral attributes thus providing some balance in participation. Therefore a support group for victims of wife battery would do well if composed of women only. But occasionally, the *goal* of the group takes precedence over the rule of "homogeneity of descriptive attributes." A group for individuals who need to learn better communication skills in marriage, for example, might do well to include both women *and* men.

Size is an issue that is generally not addressed in definitions of the term *group* except with regard to the lower limit of two (and even that has been contentious, as some fought for three as the minimum for a social unit to be designated as a group). In reviewing the writings on group size, Forsyth (1990) reports that Simmel (1902) developed a taxonomy of groups based primarily on size: a dyad has 2 members; a triad, 3; the small group, 4-20; the society, 20-30; and the large group, 40 plus. Obviously as groups increase in size, they become more complex and more capable of taking on complex tasks. Problems of interdependence also increase as size increases, so that a single-session orientation group could become too large to provide adequate response to individual members' questions.

The best size for the successful group depends on the goal of the group, the attributes of the members, the environment in which the group exists, and other variables. Discovering the "best" size may well be a matter of trial and error.

In general, this book and its discussion of group participation will focus on Simmel's "small group" (4-20), with anything more than nine beginning to feel like a large small group.

SUMMARY

To summarize, this chapter has attempted to encompass an exceedingly complex subject—the meaning of the term *group* with particular reference to the successful group. That the subject is complex is due to the wide variety of groups in terms of size, composition, history, projected length of existence, closed or open status, reasons for existence, criteria for membership, phases of development through which many groups move, and the nature of operating procedures used by the group, to name just a few variables. The emphasis has been on those qualities that help a group become successful, such as effective interdependency (including attention to task and socioemotional functions) and clear and well-accepted common goals, roles, and criteria for membership. It has also attempted to alert the reader to the fact that many collections of individuals, loosely regarded as groups, may be—at best—underdeveloped groups because they lack some of the qualities of the successful group that have been described above. Underdeveloped groups are those that are not effective in terms of goal achievement and member satisfaction: Making them into successful groups requires attention to the effective use of group participation techniques discussed in this book. The rest of this chapter lists the instructional objectives of the book, then briefly describes its content. The chapter concludes with a brief description of chapter format, and a brief note describing ways to prepare for the next chapter.

OBJECTIVES OF THIS BOOK

As a result of completing this book, each reader should be able to do the following:

1. When observing a group in action, you should be able to identify correctly the techniques of group participation used by the members of the group and evaluate the degree to which these techniques have been used correctly and effectively in a way that would agree with my assessment, were I present.

2. When serving as a formally designated Group Leader, you should be able to recognize correctly when a particular technique or set of techniques should be used (i.e., be able to provide a rationale for the selection of particular techniques), then use the technique(s) so that the desired outcome is achieved.

3. When participating as a group member, you should be able to recognize correctly when a particular technique or set of techniques should be used, then use the technique(s) so that the desired outcome is achieved.

CONTENT OF THIS BOOK

The book focuses on specific techniques only[6] and makes no pretense of covering such topics as group composition, individual assessment of potential members, the use of program activities in groups, and so on. In short, it is viewed as a component part of a larger educational effort. The following techniques are discussed:

1. *Attending:* letting others in a group know that you are paying close attention to what they say and do[7]
2. *Information Management:* asking questions and giving information in a group
3. *Contract Negotiation:* working out an agreement on goals for the group and its members, and the ground rules to be used in working toward these goals as a group.[8]
4. *Rewarding:* providing payoffs—such as praise—for effort and/or achievement in a group
5. *Responding to Feeling:* letting others in a group know that you accurately understand how they feel about a situation
6. *Focusing:* keeping a group discussion on track
7. *Summarizing:* pulling together what has been said by group participants for review and as a basis for next steps
8. *Gatekeeping:* achieving a balance of participation in a group, by inviting low participators to speak up, and limiting high participators
9. *Confrontation:* informing a participant, subgroup, or the entire group about discrepancies in words and actions to require that they consider these inconsistencies.[9]
10. *Modeling:* teaching by demonstration, learning by imitation
11. *Mediating:* attempting to resolve conflicts among group participants
12. *Starting:* beginning a group's first meeting and each group meeting thereafter.[10]

CHAPTER FORMAT

Each chapter describes one technique of group participation: what the technique is, when to use it, how to use it, and how to tell if it is achieving its teaching objective. There is a discussion of the technique in relation to oppression and empowerment. This is followed by a short scripted skit that depicts a group leader and group members using the technique on which the chapter focuses. Next, there are exercises that could be used by a course instructor (or staff developer) to provide opportunities for readers to practice that particular technique and then share their experience as another way to learn about that technique. Next, a post script: an issue that pertains to the use of the technique. This is followed by a brief note pertaining to preparations for the next chapter's exercise, designed for classes that use this text as the basis for a small group experience. Finally, there is a list of suggested readings should you want to read more about each technique. References to cited works are at the end of the book.

IN PREPARATION

For Exercise B, it would be appropriate for one or more members to bring a problem with which they want help or a controversial issue they would like to see explored. For Exercise C, you will need 3-by-5 cards. Check the description of that exercise so you can calculate the number of cards you will need.

NOTES

1. Not all definitions are this long. For example, Forsyth (1990) defines *group* as "two or more interdependent individuals who influence one another through social interaction" (p. 490).

2. The term *negative* does not mean "bad"; rather it is used to indicate that many actions in a group (i.e., disagreement) are normal and essential parts of group interaction.

3. If the chairperson still does not start the meeting, the act of asking him or her to start the meeting is simply a leadership attempt that failed.

4. This does not mean that a formal leader is unnecessary; rather, in groups with formal leaders, members share a responsibility with the leader to see that leadership acts necessary to the group's functioning are performed.

5. There may be some confusion in terms, and I certainly do not wish to compound it. When discussing someone who is formally designated, elected, or hired to conduct a group meeting, I am using Leader (with a capital "L"); some people who are not designated, elected, or hired to conduct a meeting are nevertheless informally powerful (occupy a high status) in a group and become leaders (with a small "l"). Accordingly, all the people who are participants, whether Leaders, leaders, or middle or lower status members, have the potential for performing leadership acts.

6. All of the techniques covered are applicable to the management of one-on-one interactions as well as to group interactions.

7. Attending comes first because it is basic to all other techniques.

8. Actually, all of the techniques can come into play when a contract is being negotiated, so in a sense Contract Negotiation is not a single technique. It is placed here because all groups need to deal with contracting issues early in the game. If you are participating in a learning group as a way of studying groups, please note that contracting is placed early in the book to call your attention to the contracting process that should be going on *now* within your own learning group.

9. Confrontation is placed here rather than earlier because it is more likely to work once a group has worked through its contract and has developed experience in implementing that contract.

10. Starting comes last only because some people who are interested in learning how to perform the role of formally designated Leader in a group may prefer to complete this entire training experience before actually starting their group. If so, they would be ending with a "beginning." Hopefully, this session could facilitate that next step.

SUGGESTED READINGS

Albritton, R., & Shaughnessy, T. (1990). *Developing leadership skills: A source book for librarians*. Englewood, CO: Libraries Unlimited.

Anderson, L., & Robertson, S. (1985). Group facilitation: Functions and skills. *Small Group Behavior, 16*(2), 139-156.

Bales, R. (1976). *Interaction process analysis: A method for the study of small groups*. Chicago, IL: University of Chicago Press.

Cerda, R., Nemiroff, H., & Richmond, A. (1991) Therapeutic group approaches in an inpatient facility for children and adolescents: A 15-year perspective. *Group, 15*(2), 71-80.

Health Care Education Associates. (1987). *Group leadership skills for nurse managers*. St. Louis, MO: Mosby.

Jacobs, E., Harvill, R., & Masson, R. (1988). *Group counseling: Strategies and skills*. Pacific Grove, CA: Brooks/Cole.

Johnson, D., & Johnson, F. (1991). *Group theory and group skills* (4th ed.). Boston, MA: Allyn and Bacon.

Lakey, B. (1982). Meeting facilitation: The no magic method. *Issues in Radical Therapy, 10*(4), 33-35.

Nixon, C., & Littlepage, G. (1992). Impact of meeting procedures on meeting effectiveness. *Journal of Business & Psychology, 6*(3), 361-369.

Pearson, R. (1985). A group-based training format for basic skills of small-group leadership. *Journal for Specialists in Group Work, 10*(3), 150-156.

Richter, J., Bottenberg, D., & Roberto, K. (1991). Focus group: Implications for program evaluation of mental health services. *Journal of Mental Health Administration, 18*(2), 148-153.

Wheelan, S. (1990). *Facilitating training groups: A guide to leadership and verbal intervention skills*. New York: Praeger.

White, R., & Lippet, R. (1968). Leader behavior and member reaction in three social climates. In D. Cartwright & R. Zander (Eds.), *Group dynamics, research and theory* (3rd ed., pp. 318-335). New York: Harper & Row.

Chapter 2

ATTENDING

HOW DO YOU DESCRIBE ATTENDING?

Attending is letting a group member know that you are paying close attention to what he or she is saying or doing so that he or she will be encouraged to continue. It enables you to gain additional information, as well as making you more sensitive to and aware of that member. In good Attending, attention and retention are combined; that is, you pay attention to what is said and done *and* you remember it as the interaction continues. In addition, you let the member know you have been Attending to him or her. In one-on-one contact, Attending is less difficult than in a group, where every member is entitled to your attention. Attending in a group, therefore, is more demanding simply because of the number of people to whom you must pay attention.

Attending seems such an obvious technique: Can you give an example of a situation you have seen recently in which Attending was *not* used?

_____

_____

_____

WHEN DO YOU ATTEND?

You attend when you want a member to continue talking or doing what he or she is doing so that you can gather more information, or to simply build rapport with him or her.

In regard to your example of the nonuse of Attending, what would have been appropriate timing for its use? Why do you think so?

_____

_____

_____

HOW DO YOU ATTEND?

1. Relax physically, so that you are comfortable and the member you are Attending will not feel pressured by you.

2. Look at the member you are Attending. Because you are in a group, look around at everyone from time to time.

3. Turn toward the particular member to whom you are Attending, lean forward in your chair, nod, and smile. Be encouraging.

4. Make sure he or she realizes that you are listening. When he or she has made an important point, you can restate it for emphasis. Usually saying, "yes," "right," "I understand," or even just "uh-huh" can reassure a person that you are following what he or she is saying.

5. When you are not sure you understand what has been said, restate what you think you heard.[1] If a speaker appears to think you still do not understand (e.g., shakes head, disagrees, or tries to explain), ask him or her to say it again. When he or she does, let the speaker know that this time you understand by telling him or her. If it still seems unclear, ask another member to restate what they understand the person to have said.

6. Do not pay *too* much attention to one or two members who volunteer to participate and neglect the others. If you overattend, a member may be flattered and contribute so much that he or she does not let anyone else talk. Or he or she may feel uncomfortable with too much attention and stop talking. Members who are not being attended to may either feel resentful, or they may be content to let someone else do all the work. Members may resent overattending because others repeatedly look at frequent volunteers, so you may have to make a conscious effort to distribute eye contact all around the group. Some people focus to one side of the room more easily than to the other. If you do this, make sure you can scan the group often, so that you have eye contact with every member.

Parenthetically, it should be noted that you may want to purposely underattend or ignore someone whose participation is not, in your view, helping the group or who is (again, in your opinion) participating too much.

In regard to your example in which Attending was not used, what should have been done? Why do you think so?

_____

_____

_____

HOW DO YOU KNOW
YOU ARE ATTENDING SUCCESSFULLY?

The member to whom you are Attending continues talking or doing what you want to encourage. You believe that you are getting additional, useful information. Members do not have to say or do things in an overly forceful or dramatic manner just to get the attention of others. Members do not compete for attention. They seem confident that they are being understood so they do not have to say only the things they think others want to hear.

OPPRESSION AND EMPOWERMENT
IN RELATION TO ATTENDING

Effective Attending requires paying attention to communications emanating from an individual and letting that individual know that you *are* paying attention to his or her communication. But in a sense, it also involves selective *ignoring* of certain kinds of information, when that information is judged by the group worker to be irrelevant to the topic at hand or likely to shift the focus of the group's activities. For example, in the scripted vignette that follows, the Leader[2] and the group attend to one another in a discussion of how to deal with a restrictive memo from the medical director of an institution for children with chronic intractable asthma. This memo was written because a member of the group had died, and the director was concerned that the group's strenuous participation in square dancing might lead to medical complications for other members. However, the Leader chose not to Attend to the actual death of the member, perhaps out of concern that the topic would be too upsetting for the others. Whether or not this was a valid choice is not the point: The fact is that Attending often involves selective ignoring.

But what about the fact that you fail to Attend when members have had a history of oppressive experiences? Members may accept your implied decision not to deal with what is really hurting them (i.e., not Attend) as typical of an uncaring world. But they will know that you have not been Attending to their reality. This can—and often does— happen because you are unfamiliar with the oppression your members know all too well as part of their daily existence. This is often the case when you are not a member of the particular oppressed populations with which members identify. In such situations, you have to seek education about the population with which you are working. You must continually ask yourself how what the group is doing pertains to the issues of oppression that is characteristic for this population. On the other hand, you may be aware of the oppressive experiences of members, but feel uncomfortable about handling the issues related to oppression in a group situation. The discussions of the other techniques that follow should help you if the thought of dealing with such content leaves you feeling inadequate. But first, you must be willing to Attend to their reality.

AN EXAMPLE OF ATTENDING IN A GROUP

SCENE

The Promenaders is a square dance club for young (11-13 years of age) residents of the Center for Asthmatic Children. The Center provides residential treatment for 125 children, ages 6 through 18, who have chronic intractable asthma. Its population is drawn from the entire country. The Promenaders was begun by Sam, a second-year graduate social work student who is doing his field placement at the Center. The purpose of the group is only secondarily recreational, for these are children whose illness has denied them participation in a whole range of social activities. Square dancing—a hobby of Sam's—seemed an appropriate activity for this age group: one that could build their confidence, skill, and endurance in a demanding physical activity. Members participate voluntarily. Several have been comparatively asthma-free since coming to the Center; others have had intermittent attacks, ranging from mild to severe, although not particularly associated with the square dancing itself. One member, May, also suffered from severe emphysema, but she was determined to participate in the group as much as possible.

The group began in October and was scheduled to end in April, when Sam's placement ended. One day in March, Sam arrived at the Center to be met by stunning news: May had died. It was explained to him that the medication that had helped her feel good, from time to time, had been unable to reverse the damage done to her heart by severe asthmatic attacks. A few weeks later, Dr. Snow, Medical Director of the Center, issued a memo stating that certain children could no longer participate in strenuous physical activities. The list of names included four of the Promenaders: Donald, Victor, Sue, and Betsy. The group had been planning a performance to show everyone at the center what they had learned, but without these four there could be no performance. In addition, they would be unable to attend the square dances at the local community center—an evening activity. Going to these dances had enhanced the group's status in the eyes of the other children at the Center. The group met to discuss the memo. In addition to the four members already mentioned, Rob, Ester, Priscilla, and Frank were present.

ACTION	DISCUSSION

SAM: Well, I guess you've all seen Dr. Snow's memo about "strenuous physical activities."

VICTOR: He's crazy! Just yesterday I was in field day. No asthma.

SAM: So, you think he's being too cautious?

A restatement of Victor's comment, minus the anger.

VICTOR: You better believe it! I mean—like—what he wants to do—he wants to wrap us up in cotton, just like my Mom used to do . . .

Victor confirms Sam's restatement, then amplifies his initial comment.

DONALD: I'd like to sit old Snow on a radiator and watch him melt.

ROB: Chop him up with a shovel and use the pieces for a snowball fight. Snow. Ball. Snowball. Get it?

SUE: Fun-nee! We get it, Dumb-Dumb, but we don't want it! Meanwhile, unless we do something, no show next month.

A lot of anger is being expressed—a healthy outpouring for kids who have often bottled up anger in the past.

SAM: Sounds like you're all ticked off by the memo. Sue, have you any ideas about the performance?

Sam lets the group know that he is Attending to what they are saying and then focuses on the problem they face—the performance.

DONALD: Tell him what he can do with his memo!

SUE: Donald! I was about to say before I was so stupidly interrupted by Mr. Loud Mouth Dumb-Dumb here—

DONALD: [Innocently] Who, me?

Sam purposely does *not* attend to Donald, so as to discourage his clowning.

SUE: Oh, Donald, this is serious. Can't you cut out the clowning just this once?

Sue asks Donald to attend to the business at hand

DONALD: OK, sorry.

Donald agrees and then attends to Sue's request.

SUE: Well, I was about to say— uh—that—[finishes lamely] I don't know what we should do.

Sue indicates she has attended to Sam's question, but she has no suggestions.

SAM: Priscilla, you look like you've got an idea.

Sam attends to Priscilla's nonverbal cue that she wants to speak.

PRISCILLA: Do you think he would let us do just the performance and then stop?

SAM: In other words, continue to rehearse for the performance? But you didn't say anything about the dances at the Center.

Sam restates Priscilla's comment; one form of Attending.

PRISCILLA: Oh, well, I mean, we'd stop going to those. So, we would be cutting back.

FRANK: Yeah. And maybe we could tell him that we'd cut out some of the dances in the performance and not let the ones we do run so long. And we would sing more songs than we were going to, instead of dancing.

Frank shows he has been Attending by adding to Priscilla's suggestion.

VICTOR: I don't like that, no way! We've done pretty good in this group. I mean—uh—nobody's had a bad attack from dancing. If I start feeling bad, I just sit down for a while. And I can keep going longer than I used to. If we cut back—well, it'll be like I never had done better.

SAM: And that would make you feel like you're right back where you started?

Here Sam attends to Victor's fear that he will lose the progress he made.

VICTOR: Right. Only worse, 'cause I tried and failed.

ESTER: But Victor—well, I know how you feel, but Dr. Snow's worried because of May . . .

VICTOR: I understand what he's worried about. And I guess it's his job to worry. When May—well, it was sad, you know. And it was scary, too, 'cause it seemed like she was doing better and all. But you can't let things like that run your life. . . .

Sam allowed the discussion to move into the areas of trying to expand one's ability to operate within the confines of asthma, and then asked the group to focus on the memo. Eventually it was decided that the group as a whole would request a meeting with Dr. Snow to see if some way could be found for them to continue the group until the performance.

EXERCISES

EXERCISE A

This exercise may seem so obvious, so simplistic, that you are tempted to skip it. Don't. It makes a basic point that you cannot afford to ignore.

Goals (for exercises A and B)

When participating in a group meeting, you will be able to use Attending behavior in such a way that every other member of the group would say (if asked) that he or she believed you had been paying attention to him or her.

Time Required

About 20 minutes

Process

Break into subgroups of three or four. Each subgroup should be far enough apart so as not to interfere with the other subgroups.

Designate one member of each subgroup to be an active Attender in the first part of this exercise.

Have a 5-minute conversation in the subgroup during which the Attender actively uses Attending behavior for the first 3 minutes. The discussion could be about why the members are in this class, how each sees it fitting into his or her career plans, how learning to work in or with groups is important to their future jobs, or some other topic, selected by the instructor. After 3 minutes, the instructor should signal the Attender in each group to *stop Attending* while the conversation continues for another 2 minutes.

Change roles so that all members are designated as "Attender" and repeat the process.

Reassemble the class and discuss your experiences. What happened when the Attender stopped Attending? What significance does this experience have for the role of leadership in a group? How do members respond to being ignored? And so forth.

EXERCISE B (An optional additional exercise)

Select a controversial topic in which the group is likely to be interested and on which students are known to have different points of view. Ask two members who honestly disagree to be forceful spokespersons for these opposing points of view. Each spokesperson (A, then B) is to be given a minute or two to make an introductory statement supporting his or her viewpoint. From that point, let the group members join in, addressing their questions or comments to *any* member, not just the spokesperson. But here is the catch: Before anyone can speak, he or she has to briefly restate the gist of what the person who spoke *just before* has said *to that person's satisfaction*. Remember: The previous speaker has to be satisfied that his or her position, comment, or question has been restated (i.e., attended to) correctly before the new speaker can make his or her own statement. If the new speaker has not attended correctly to what was said, he or she must work to find a restatement that satisfies the previous speaker. And after the new speaker has satisfied the previous speaker and then made his or her own statement, the *next* speaker must restate the just-previous-speaker's position, and so on. (The only ones who are excused from this obligation of restatement are the two spokespersons—A and B—and *only* when they make their *first* position statements. Thereafter, spokespersons must restate what has gone before.) See how far the group gets in discussing the topic, then discuss the experience. What kinds of statements were easier to restate? Harder? What are the implications of your observations for participation in group discussions either as a leader or member? Complete the exercise and discussion before reading further.

Comments on Exercise B

Exercise B may have shown you that we do not always use good Attending behavior in a group in which a topic that is meaningful to us is being discussed. The study of semantics, the meaning of language, has amply demonstrated that we use many words that mean different things to different people; for example, "relationship," "democracy," and "freedom," to mention but a few. Attending can be particularly difficult to do in a group, compared to a one-on-one exchange; it takes a lot of practice. This is particularly true when the topic of discussion is emotionally charged, as in the discussion of opposing points of view.

EXERCISE C (Another optional exercise)

Select one group member as the first subject (S) of this exercise. (Draw lots, accept a volunteer, or use some other procedure.) Every member is to write on a 3-by-5 card (a) one thing about S's view of today's class that they think has been satisfying to S and (b) one thing about the class that they think has been dissatisfying to S. Whenever possible, rely on more than S's stated opinions—S's facial expressions for example. Keep these statements as brief as possible; aim for one sentence about S's satisfaction and one about S's dissatisfaction. Give all of the written statements to S, let S read them silently, select those he or she wishes to discuss, and then comment on the degree to which the statements are in fact accurate reflections of his or her thinking. Because accuracy of members' observations of S (rather than a confrontation of attitudes of which S might be unaware) is what is being practiced here, S has the right to decide which, if any, of the statements he or she wants to discuss in the group. Then discuss the *kinds of evidence* participants used to ascertain what S was thinking or feeling. You should then go clockwise around the class and repeat the exercise, giving as many other students the chance to assume the S role as time will allow.

SUMMARY

If you are using this book as the basis of a self-managed group, you can use the time at the end of a class session in a variety of ways.

- If one member was designated as a nonparticipating observer, he or she can use this time to present feedback on the class's interaction processes for discussion.
- Students could be asked to summarize the major points of the session.
- Students could work out assignments for the next class; for example, what might be read prior to the next session, what could be done in preparation for the next session, and so on.

POSTSCRIPT: ISSUES IN ATTENDING

As you go through these materials, you will find that each technique can serve numerous functions. For example, you Attend in order to Seek Information or Respond to Feelings, you Mediate in order to Summarize, you Seek Information in order to Mediate, and so on. So let us look at some of the multiple functions of Attending and some of the complexities this suggests.

Essentially, Attending can be a powerful reward. If a Leader and/or other member attends to you appropriately in a group, you are likely to increase your participation in that group. If the Leader or other member persists in not Attending to you, after a while you will give up trying to get their attention (although you might initially try working harder to get that attention). But Attending in a group serves several other functions. For example, I attend in order to provide a model of good Attending behavior for group members; that is, I want them to imitate me and attend to one another. But they might make the mistake of Attending only to me, instead of to one another, which would not be beneficial to group development. So when members do appear to be Attending to one another, an effective Leader would reward such behavior by praising it.

We attend not simply to reward another's participation but to better understand that person; that is, to gather data about him or her that he or she generates and that we try to comprehend. We hear what someone actually says, recognizing that what he or she says is often not what he or she is thinking. For example, a person may promise to do something, but may not keep that promise. We listen for covert as well as overt content, as in the following examples:

- The person who speaks about people in authority who have been unreliable, so that you begin to suspect that he or she may be asking you, indirectly, whether you will make promises like all the others, without following through
- The person who curses in your presence not because he or she is angry but in order to test your response
- The person who tells you that he or she feels pretty good about something while nervously twisting a paper clip with his or her hands

The exercises should have demonstrated that Attending is more than common courtesy. In fact, *courtesy is what we often substitute for active Attending.* For example, how often do you discover that you have already forgotten the name of someone you just met, although you followed all the rules of etiquette when you were introduced?

The problem in Attending is that we are faced with so much information that we must block some of it out. The famous fictional detective, Sherlock Holmes, attributed much of his success to his acute powers of observation. To make his point, he asked his old friend, Dr. Watson, how many steps one had to climb to reach their flat at 221-B Baker Street. Although Watson had climbed these stairs innumerable times, he had to admit that he did not know how many steps there were.

Attending in a group is complicated by the fact that one tries to "read" both verbal and nonverbal bits of information from several people at once. As you work to improve your group participation skills, however, you will learn that Attending is the *basic* technique, without which all else fails, and that to improve your Attending you will have to make a conscious effort to overcome the self-protecting, nonattending habits you have acquired over the years.

IN PREPARATION

No particular preparation is needed for the next session.

NOTES

1. This is really a form of Information Seeking, which will be covered in the next chapter. It is important to note the interconnectedness of all the techniques and the fact that Attending is basic to all of the other techniques.

2. Throughout the book "leader" and "worker" are used interchangeably.

SUGGESTED READINGS

Dickson, D., & Mullan, T. (1990). An empirical investigation of the effects of a micro-counseling programmed with social work students: The acquisition and transfer of component skills. *Counseling Psychology Quarterly, 3*(3), 267-283.

Gochros, H. (1985-1986). Overcoming resistance to talking about sex. *Journal of Social Work and Human Sexuality, 4*(1-2), 7-15.

Ivey, A. (1991). *Development strategies for helpers: Individual, family, and network interventions.* Pacific Grove, CA: Brooks/Cole.

Ivey, A., Ivey, M., & Simek-Downing, M. (1987). *Counseling and psychotherapy: Integrating skills, theory and practice.* Englewood Cliffs, NJ: Prentice Hall.

Kendall, P., & Braswell, L. (1986). Medical applications of cognitive-behavioral interventions with children. *Journal of Developmental and Behavioral Pediatrics, 7*(4), 257-264.

Rix, K. (1988). Teaching a mother to attend differentially to her mental handicapped child's behaviour. *Behavioral Psychotherapy, 16*(2), 122-132.

Shag, D., Loo, C., & Levin, M. (1978). The group assessment of interpersonal traits (GAIT): Differentiation of measures and their relationship to behavioral response modes. *American Journal of Community Psychology, 6*(1), 47-62.

Chapter 3

SEEKING AND GIVING INFORMATION

HOW DO YOU DESCRIBE INFORMATION SEEKING AND INFORMATION GIVING?

Information Seeking and Information Giving are presented together to highlight their similarities and differences.

Similar to Attending, they appear to involve a fairly obvious set of techniques until you remember how poorly we often handle them. For instance, how often do people ask a question, then attempt to clarify the first question by restating it, so that they actually change the kind of information being sought? And surely you have been oriented to a new job, a new class, or a new responsibility with so much information that you could not retain most of it, or worse, with a lot of verbiage but no clear information you could use? We are dealing here with a range of problems related to communication: different language patterns and styles, a range of listening skills, differential ability to absorb and retain information, fear of disclosing private information about oneself when asked personal questions, and so forth.

INFORMATION SEEKING

Information Seeking is an attempt to add new information (facts, knowledge) to what you already know. You can ask group members questions: what they know or think are the facts about a particular issue, situation, or event. Sometimes you get information by making statements (such as, "So in this kind of situation, you would have done . . .") in such a way that a member's agreement or disagreement reflects his or her knowledge. The term *Information Seeking* does not refer to all questions; only to those related to an individual's perception of facts (as differentiated from the individual's opinions and feelings). In effect, Information Seeking can be defined as asking one or more participants to give information; that is, give facts or whatever knowledge about a topic is available as it is known to them.

What is an example of Information Seeking in a group that you've experienced recently?

_____

_____

_____

_____

INFORMATION GIVING

Information Giving involves giving the group what the information giver thinks are *facts* or *knowledge available* about the topic on which the group is working. The term *facts* distinguishes this behavior from opinion-giving or making suggestions. For example,

Information Giving: "Company X turned down 10 out of the last 10 applicants with a prison record that we sent them."

Opinion: "Personally, I think Company X is prejudiced against ex-prisoners."

Suggestion: "If I were you, I wouldn't tell Company X about my prison record unless I thought they were really interested in hiring me, and I really wanted their job."

Information to be information should be confirmable; that is, there should be some way of proving that Company X, referred to above, did turn down 10 out of the last 10 applicants with prior prison records. Otherwise, what is being communicated may be opinion or suggestion rather than fact or knowledge.

What is an example of Information Giving in a group that you have recently experienced?

_____

_____

_____

WHEN DO YOU USE INFORMATION SEEKING AND INFORMATION GIVING?

INFORMATION SEEKING

To solve problems. You seek information when the group is trying to solve a problem and information that is necessary for reaching a solution is lacking, or when the group's information appears to be inaccurate. Further, you seek information when the group is ready to solve a problem or resolve an issue on the basis of opinion or flimsy data. It is always a good idea to seek information before taking action, rather than acting solely on the basis of opinion or feeling. Often there is no confirmable information, but even knowing that there is no information is helpful, because it suggests that your action should be tentative, at least until some information about the results of your action is available.

To get to know one another. You seek information (e.g., work experiences, areas of competence, etc.) when participants do not know enough about one another to invest in relationships with one another.

To achieve clarity of communication. You seek information when you suspect that participants have inaccurate ideas about what is expected or that their definitions for

INFORMATION GIVING

To solve problems. You give information when it is clear from what a member is saying that he or she has incomplete or inaccurate information. This is indicated by pointless arguments and off-topic discussions or too-early closure when dealing with a complicated issue. Ideally, participants should ask for the correct information, but if they do not and you have it, it should be offered. It is important to give information when it can be put to use; if given too far in advance, it may be forgotten.

To get to know one another. You give information when you (either as group Leader or member) believe that it would be helpful for the group to know something about yourself (e.g., your expertise, experiences, interests, etc.) or information that you possess about other members of the group.

To achieve clarity of communication. You give information when you want to be sure members understand what you are saying, by defining your use of terms are different from yours (or some of the members) and you want to know how certain things are perceived.

To receive feedback. You seek feedback when you want others to tell you how they perceive what you are doing as a group Leader or member. Here the line between information and opinion is likely to be fuzzy, at best.

In regard to your example of Information Seeking, was it sought at the right time? Why do you think so?

of terms or by giving examples of what you mean.

To give feedback. You give information when a Leader or member is trying to learn a new or different way of behaving, and you want him or her to know how well he or she is doing by comparing his or her behavior to specific goals.

In regard to your example of Information Giving, was it given at the right time? Why do you think so?

_____

_____

_____

_____

_____

_____

HOW DO YOU MANAGE
SEEKING AND GIVING INFORMATION?

INFORMATION SEEKING

Using the group. When information is needed, encourage members to seek the information from one another. Avoid situations in which all information questions are asked by the group's Leader.

INFORMATION GIVING

Using the group. When giving information, remember that the best sources of information are the group members themselves. Even when the Leader knows the facts, he or she should first try to discover if one or more of the members has the information, and, if so, ask that person or persons to give it. This helps to increase the confidence of group members in their group and in themselves. The Leader, however, should provide or locate the information when it is needed to keep discussion moving, if trying to elicit it from members appears to them as "playing group games."

Simple familiar language. Ask only one question at a time. Then wait for an answer. Then listen. Make sure you are Attending. Avoid asking such long complicated questions that others will not understand what you are asking.

Simple familiar language. Give information briefly and in a way that is easily understood and remembered. Use words that are familiar to members, provide brief written handouts, and so on. If you have a lot of information, give the most important piece of information first, as it is more likely to be remembered. In addition, try to present discrete pieces of information as part of a small number of categories, first explaining the logic of those categories.

"Yes" or "No" Answers. Avoid asking questions that can be answered by "Yes" or "No" because that cuts off discussion. The exception is when you want to pin down particular information and believe a yes/no answer will help you do so.

"Yes" or "No" Answers. I said be brief but a "Yes" or "No" answer is usually too brief, unless it is to confirm that the information seeker has phrased his or her question in such a way as to show that he or she already has the information and simply wants you to confirm that fact.

Reasons for seeking the information. When seeking information, tell the information giver why you want it and how you plan to use it. Otherwise, he or she may be unwilling to give you the information freely.

Reasons for giving the information. When giving information, make sure that the information being given is relevant to the purpose of the group and/or the needs of one or more members. If it is not immediately obvious, tell the group why you are giving the information.

Tone of voice. Ask the questions in a neutral way so that the person does not feel pushed to answer in a particular way. For example, avoid sarcasm, disbelief, and so on.

In the example of Information Seeking that you described, was the information sought effectively? Why do you think so?

—————————————————

—————————————————

—————————————————

—————————————————

Tone of voice. Avoid an overly positive statement of the facts, as they are known to you. Otherwise, you may cut off further discussion by people who have different information from yours.

In your example of Information Giving, was the information given effectively? Why do you think so?

—————————————————

—————————————————

—————————————————

—————————————————

HOW DO YOU KNOW YOU HAVE USED INFORMATION SEEKING OR INFORMATION GIVING CORRECTLY?

INFORMATION SEEKING

Group. The members of the group agree that the information being sought is what is needed to help solve the problem and/or finish the task being done.

Feedback. You receive information that you believe will help you to perform more effectively as a member or a Leader.

INFORMATION GIVING

Group. The members of the group agree that the information given is correct and sufficiently complete to help solve the problem and/or finish the task being done.

Feedback. In giving feedback, the member or Leader who receives the feedback will continue correct behavior and modify incorrect behavior so that he or she performs acceptably well in relation to individual and/or group goals.

OPPRESSION AND EMPOWERMENT
IN RELATION TO SEEKING
AND GIVING INFORMATION

In Solomon's (1992) discussion of clinical diagnosis among diverse populations, she makes the point that

> behavior that is considered dysfunctional or abnormal in the dominant culture may be functional and normal in another culture . . . Institutional racism may cause misdiagnosis; for example, it has been argued that the Diagnostic and Statistical Manual of Mental Disorders-III-R (DSM-III-R) contains inherent assumptions that reflect a Western bias. Clinicians must examine their own prejudices so that assessment procedures can better reflect the reality of their clients' experience.

Given this issue, one has to wonder: Do the questions I choose to ask reflect my own assumptions—assumptions that are "out of sync" with a client's about the nature of the world? When this occurs, clients know or sense this discrepancy. The result may be that they give an answer that they know you want to hear, but that they believe makes no sense to them.

It is often the case that people are not familiar with their own prejudices. At the University of Michigan, students learn about their prejudgments and lack of correct information about people from other populations by meeting in "dialogue groups" that purposely combine people from two populations (e.g., black/white, male/female, gay/straight, etc.) and—with the help of facilitators who meet with a group of 8-12 over the course of several weeks—learn about others, and learn about themselves. It is always a powerful—and often upsetting—experience, but the participants and facilitators generally find it useful.

Similarly, in giving information, one has to be aware of one's own assumptions about what others want to hear. Every teacher who cares about the instructional process is aware of a classroom situation in which students withhold negative comments for fear of inviting an instructor's wrath. In such situations, these students listen and do what they must do to pass the course then they depart without really incorporating the information dispensed into their own "warehouse" of knowledge that they believe is useful to acquire and retain. Again, awareness of one's own assumptions about the population being addressed can help one avoid this pitfall.

AN EXAMPLE OF SEEKING AND
GIVING INFORMATION IN A GROUP

SCENE

The Job Club is a program for job seekers and new job holders sponsored by the State Department of Labor. The group has a dual purpose: (a) to help prepare people who are seeking employment to engage in effective job search behaviors, and (b) once employed, to help these same people through early on-the-job problems. The group comprises eight young adult members (ages 18-28), including Carmen, who recently began working as a file clerk in a U.S. Army Recruiting Office, and Phil, who has been working at the County Hospital as an attendant for about a month and a half. All eight members joined the Club two months ago, but two members have not as yet found jobs. The members meet in an unused meeting room in the basement of City Hall. Mrs. Edwards is the first group leader to be used in this program. This club is an experiment to test the usefulness of the Job Club idea. The group meets weekly from 7:30 p.m. to 9:00 p.m. so that members can either look for jobs during the day or report on the jobs they have heard about and/or for which they have applied. Attendance has been surprisingly regular, suggesting that the group is achieving its dual purpose, in the opinion of the group's members.

ACTION	DISCUSSION
CARMEN: So this corporal, he waits until the sergeant is out of the office on his lunch break and then he starts in with his—uh, "Hey, Carmen, I'm going to blow in your ear. Hey, what'll you do when I blow in your ear?" And all like that. And what I mean is he ain't got no right to talk to me like that. I mean, like, it really bugs me!	Carmen gives information about her problem. When the sergeant is out, she reports, the men flirt with her, and it bothers her.
VERA: Yeah, well, so, what did you say? I mean, like, you know, how did you feel when he said that?	Vera asks two questions at once.

MRS. EDWARDS: Let's take those questions one at a time, OK? So, Carmen, what did you do when the corporal said that?

The worker breaks Vera's two-part question into two questions and restates Vera's first question.

CARMEN: I told him he better not! Like, I mean, I can take it when guys horse around, you know. But sometimes they go too far. And, I mean, sometimes I want some respect, you know. But it's all the time—this— "Gonna-blow-in-your-ear" jazz that really gets me mad! All the time. All the time! "Car-men! Gonna blow in your ee-ear!"

Mrs. Edwards knows that this may be a serious case of sexual harassment, or it simply may be the kind of testing many new employees have to face.

MRS. EDWARDS: Phil, doesn't that sound a little like what's been happening to you at the hospital? I don't mean "Blow in your ear"—just harassment that really can be annoying.

Mrs. Edwards asks Phil to give information about his situation in order to draw attention to the general problem new employees face when harassed by other employees.

PHIL: Yeah—well—yeah, I guess so. I mean all the time, you know, the nurses' aides, they're always teasing me. "Hey, Phil, bet all the girls are crazy about you with your big brown eyes and that long curly hair." It bothered me at first until I figured it out, that they were just riding me 'cause I was new. So I'd tease 'em right back and say, "Yeah, it's rough having to fight off all those women single-handed! But that's OK," I'd say, "If you ladies want to get on my list you can join the crowd." And stuff like that. And pretty soon they just stopped.

Phil describes the female-male teasing he got as a new employee and how he successfully dealt with it. He gives brief, to-the-point, useful information, that proves far better than a lengthy exposition by Mrs. Edwards on the testing a new employee is likely to encounter.

CARMEN: Well, maybe that would work for you, but if I told one of them to come on over and blow in my ear, I'd really be in trouble. I mean, I don't mind having the guys notice me, but they go too far!

Carmen has heard what Phil said but is not sure how to use the information.

MRS. EDWARDS: OK, I think we're beginning to get some idea of what's bothering Carmen. But I'm wondering what else we need to know about her situation before we try figuring out some answers for her?

Mrs. Edwards delays moving to possible solution strategies too early—the group needs to seek more information from Carmen before they can generate possible solutions that are based on a good understanding of her situation.

As the discussion continued, it became clear to the group that Carmen was ambivalent about the attention she was receiving. Members offered many suggestions to her about how to avoid or deal with the testing while maintaining a good relationship with the others in the office. In reflecting on the meeting, Mrs. Edwards decided that the other members had profited from the discussion, particularly those still looking for, or about to start a job, but that Carmen would probably need further help from the group regarding this situation. So she made a mental note to ask Carmen about the problem at the next meeting.

EXERCISE

Goals

When participating in a group meeting, you will be able to *seek* information in a way that causes other members to respond, as fully as they can, with information that is relevant to the group's goal(s). In addition, you will be able to *give* information in a way that other members would say (if asked) added to the group's ability to achieve its goals.

Depending on the nature of the group doing this exercise, a larger purpose of this exercise is to increase members' knowledge about one another's similarities and differences so as to facilitate future interactions in the group.

Time Required

About 30 minutes

Materials

None

Specialized Roles

Divide the group into subgroups of three members. Each member is to play the role of Information Seeker in the subgroup for 5 minutes. If you have one or two members left over, add them singly to existing subgroups and give them a turn in the Information Seeker role.

Process

Each Information Seeker is to attempt to find out as much information as possible about the other persons in his or her subgroup, given the time limit of 5 minutes: where they come from; what kinds of work experiences they have had; what their interest, skills, or hobbies are; and any other information that the Information Seeker thinks will be helpful for the development of the larger group. The Information Seeker should try to conduct the interview without taking any written notes. Subgroup participants who are being queried should attempt to use good Information Giving behaviors in replying to the Information Seeker.

Once this process is completed in each subgroup, bring the entire group together again and share the information you have acquired about one another; that is, go around the group and have the Information Seekers relate what they learned about the person(s) they interviewed, allowing the person(s) to correct inaccurate or incomplete information.

Now review the process you have just gone through: what worked, what did not; did anyone feel that they were being inappropriately probed for information; what was a particularly good question; and so forth. For example, did one person's manner of seeking information elicit more or different kinds of responses than someone else's? Did you have difficulty differentiating information from opinion? What kinds of information were more likely to be retained or lost, and why? When you have concluded your discussion, move to a summary of the session.

POSTSCRIPT: ISSUES IN INFORMATION EXCHANGE

In the discussion of group composition, in Chapter 1, I described the ways in which members' *descriptive attributes* can impact on group participation. In this chapter, you read about a number of ways to facilitate the exchange of information in a group. Key to this process is a recognition that an individual's descriptive attributes can affect his or her willingness to *trust* others with private information.

It is my sense that individuals who share attributes that are associated with membership in oppressed populations are often distrustful of others whose attributes identify them as possible oppressors. Adolescents may automatically distrust adults; African Americans are likely to distrust whites; the physically disabled are likely to distrust the healthy person; "gays" are likely to distrust "straights"; and so on.

Without trust, accurate and complete information exchange is unlikely. In some cases, this issue is less intrusive when everyone in the group, including its formal leaders, shares the attribute of membership in an oppressed group. But where this is not the case and descriptive attributes are mixed, the issue of trust/distrust in relation to member attributes should be openly acknowledged and discussed. The next chapter, on Contract Negotiation, focuses on a process in which such discussion *should* take place, but the issue will not be resolved simply because it is formally addressed, once, when the group negotiates its contract. Rather, the issue of trust will exist throughout the life of the group and should be referred to repeatedly, particularly when members find that their group is not being as successful as they would like it to be.

Trust is defined as a "firm belief in the honesty, truthfulness, justice, or power of a person or thing; faith (World Book Dictionary, 1971, p. 2228). Achieving trust in a group is never easy.

IN PREPARATION

For the Contract Negotiation exercises you will need an audiotape (or videotape) cassette recorder and a blank tape. Depending on where you meet, you may also need an extension cord or a machine that is battery operated. Check it out.

SUGGESTED READINGS

Amir, M. (1988). How does the physician decide about giving information to cancer patients? *Megamot, 31*(2), 152-166.

Atkinson, D. (1988). Research interviews with people with mental handicaps. *Mental Handicap Research, 1*(1), 75-90.

Bunce, B. (1991). Referential communication skills: Guidelines for therapy. *Language, Speech and Hearing Skills in Schools, 22*(1), 296-301.

Duffy, G., Roehler, L., Meloth, M., & Vavrus, L. (1986). Conceptualizing instructional explanation. *Teaching and Teacher Education, 2*(3), 197-214.

Fishbein, H. (1992). Teacher versus learner controlled instruction: Question-asking and comprehension. *British Journal of Educational Psychology, 62*(1), 126-131.

Galbraith, M. (Ed.). (1991). *Facilitating adult learning: A transactional process.* Malabar, FL: Krieger.

Goldstein, F., & Levin, H. (1991). Question-asking strategies after severe closed head injury. *Brain and Cognition, 17*(1), 23-30.

Hjelm-Karlsson, K. (1989). Comparison of oral, written and audio-visually based information as preparation for intravenous pyelography. *International Journal of Nursing Studies, 26*(1), 53-68.

Lauer, T., & Peacock, E. (1990). An analysis of comparison questions in the context of auditing. *Discourse Processes, 13*(3), 349-361.

McKillip, J., Moirs, K., & Cervenka, C. (1992). Asking open-ended consumer questions to aid program planning: Variations in question format and length. *Evaluation and Program Planning, 15*(1), 1-6.

Moss, S., Marquison, F., & Godbert, K. (1991). The maintenance of psychotherapy skill acquisition: A two-year follow-up. *British Journal of Medical Psychology, 64*(3), 233-236.

Ragan, S., & Pagano, M. (1987). Communicating with female patients: Affective interaction during contraceptive counseling and gynecologic exams. *Women's Studies in Communication, 10*(2), 46-57.

Roter, D., Lipkin, M., & Korsgaard, A. (1991). Sex differences in patients' and physicians' communication during primary care medical visits. *Medical Care, 29*(11), 1083-1093.

Street, R. (1991). Information-giving in medical consultations: The influence of parents' communication styles and personal characteristics. *Social Science and Medicine, 32*(5), 541-548.

Verhaak, P., & Van Bussbach, J. (1988). Patient education in general practice. *Patient Education and Counseling, 11*(2), 119-129.

Verhulst, J., & Van de Vijver, F. (1990). Resistance during psychotherapy and behavior therapy. *Behavior Modification, 4*(2), 172-187.

Chapter 4

CONTRACT NEGOTIATION

HOW DO YOU DESCRIBE CONTRACT NEGOTIATION?

The term *contract*, as used here, refers first to an explicitly stated agreement to abide by specified and relatively certain norms in order to obtain a more predictable relationship among members of a group and between each member and the group Leader(s). Second, a contract specifies the goal(s) that the group as a whole and/or its individual members hope to achieve through their participation in the group. All parties to a contract have the right and responsibility to know about and negotiate details of such an agreement, rather than assuming that the agreement is implicit, well-understood, and acceptable to all. The expectations to which people agree become implied contractual obligations.

Accordingly, *Contract Negotiation* refers to the discussions that involve group members and the formal group Leader(s) (where such leadership exists) in deciding about the expectations they have for one another and for the group as a whole.

There are so many different kinds of groups that the types of contracts groups can, or do, negotiate vary widely. For example, members of a board of education interact according to a set of bylaws; members of a basketball team interact according to prescriptions set forth by their coach and by the rules of the game; members of a social club often begin their group with no contract other than the social amenities prescribed by their culture; and so on. The discussion that follows assumes that participants are more likely to be satisfied with a group if they can influence the nature of its contract throughout the life of the group.

What is an example of Contract Negotiation in a group that you have recently seen?

_____

_____

_____

_____

WHEN DO YOU NEGOTIATE A CONTRACT?

In some groups, a preliminary contract is negotiated between the group Leader (assuming there is one) and with each potential member *before* he or she becomes a full-fledged member of the group. Obviously, real-life conditions may make it difficult, if not impossible, to work out a contract before the first meeting of the group; nevertheless, when it can be effected, a preliminary contract *should be negotiated with each potential member.*

In some groups (for example, a treatment group) the negotiation of the secondary contract between the individual group members and the group Leader, and among the group members themselves, begins during the first meeting, at which time a tentative plan of operation is worked out. In some cases, a highly specific set of agreements is reached in the first meeting, but it often takes more than one meeting to establish an effective working contract, especially when a group is meeting for the first time and is composed of strangers. Because the group is likely to change over time, it will probably be necessary to renegotiate parts of the contract throughout the life of the group. As membership changes, new members need to be informed about the nature of the group's existing contract. From time to time, regardless of the degree to which membership changes, the group should review its contract to keep it relevant to the group's circumstances.

Do you think that the process of Contract Negotiation you have described was carried out at the right time? Why do you think so?

_____

_____

_____

_____

HOW DO YOU NEGOTIATE A CONTRACT?

Before discussing the negotiation of a contract, it would be beneficial to make explicit a few assumptions that underlie the decision to use a group. It is assumed that (a) The purpose of the group is consistent with the purpose(s) and nature of your organization; that is, it is not attempting to achieve something that your organization, by its very nature, cannot deliver. (b) The group members have the kind of concerns, interests, or needs for which the group is designed. (c) Different kinds of groups, as mentioned above, allow differing degrees of freedom for negotiation. For example, a task group, such as a board of directors that has existed for some time and has operated according to a set of bylaws presents a different picture than a new group, such as a support group composed of people who do not know one another who are suffering from the same disease. In the discussion that follows, greater attention is paid to the latter group. You negotiate a contract by focusing on the following issues, though not necessarily in any particular order.

GOALS

The group Leader (or, in a group with no Leader, the person(s) who convened the group) usually begins by describing the intended goals and nature of this group in general terms—general, so that members can make the group focus on *its* specific concerns. Members should be invited to discuss the suggested goals as well as to make their own suggestions. Group members should be able to arrive at a number of goals that are of interest to them and are agreed upon by all who are present, including the Leader (if there is one). A good way to find out if everyone understands these goals is to ask one or more group members to restate them in his or her own words and then verify what has been said by asking the others if this agrees with their view of what has been said. Another possibility is to write them on a chalkboard, if one is available, or on large sheets of newsprint. The newsprint has an advantage because it can be saved for review at a later date so that the group can compare its situation at that time with its original goals. Eventually, these goals will need to be stated in specific terms to provide criteria for measuring progress toward goals. For example, in a treatment group, goals are negotiated in terms of what each member should be able to do to some measurable degree in relation to some problematic condition of his or hers. In a committee, goals are negotiated in terms of what the group hopes to accomplish in relation to the committee's charge. In a case conference group, representatives of several organizations negotiate the kinds of results they hope the group will accomplish in relation to the needs of their respective organizations.

ROLES

The group Leader (or a convening member) describes and discusses his or her expectations about the operation of the group. This includes telling the group what they can and cannot expect of her or him, what he or she would like to be able to expect of them, and what they could or should expect of each other, that is, their *roles*. Members should understand that their roles include being helpful to one another by doing such things as listening, giving suggestions, seeking or giving information that might be useful, giving support, and so on. The Leader's role expectations for the members, or the expectations they have for one another, may or may not fit those held by some of the members; this must be discussed and worked out whenever it is clear that expectations do not mesh. If this is a group with no formal leader, members should discuss what they would like to expect from one another, and from themselves, to achieve consensus on these expectations.

CRITERIA

It is extremely important that the participants have a clear idea of what it is they are trying to do (goals) and how they will know when they have done it (criteria). For example, in civil service exams, a passing score on a test is the criterion by which the degree of goal achievement is measured. Situations that require subjective criteria are problematic: To establish criteria in such areas will entail discussion leading to group consensus. Criteria must be as measurable as possible, as well as being meaningful to the participants. Be careful not to let the Leader or some group members impose criteria on the group without everyone's agreement to them.

PAYOFF

At some point in the contract discussion, the group should enumerate the types of payoffs that are available to or desired by the members as a result of participating in the group; for example, getting hired, being able to elicit a more positive response from others, having the organization accept the committee's recommendations, and so forth. Although some payoffs are tangible, such as praise from others and getting paid, others are less visible but no less important, such as the feeling of pride that goes with mastery of a new skill or the sense of satisfaction that comes from helping someone else succeed. Again, it should be mentioned that specification of and agreement about what the payoffs can be is essential in a group. To neglect such agreements may mean, for example, that what the Leader thinks are payoffs are not thought of as such by some members. This could strongly affect their participation.

During Contract Negotiation it helps to summarize from time to time to make sure that the contract is still understood and agreed upon (see the chapter on Summarizing). Whenever members do not agree, they will probably have to back up and rework whatever is being discussed so that a particular goal, role expectation, criterion, or payoff becomes acceptable to all concerned. This may mean trying to find ways of achieving clarity, looking for a compromise among different positions, agreeing to postpone a decision on the particular issue to an agreed-upon time, or recognizing that certain factors are "givens" and cannot be negotiated.

Contracts have many parts to them; agreement to a contract does not mean that members will remember all the elements. If the group has a Leader, it will be helpful for him or her to restate relevant portions in future meetings when the occasion arises. For example, when one member makes a helpful suggestion to another, in the next meeting the Leader could say something like, "Last time we agreed that we would try to help each other, and it's good to see we're doing that," or "I can see you don't agree with his point of view, but we did agree to let everyone have their say."

Groups sometimes find that a written contract is more useful and binding than a spoken one because specifics can be recorded rather than forgotten. This may be particularly important when the contract is complex or the group is composed of representatives of other groups. In some cases, members may agree to sign a contract to make their commitment to its terms, as well as to make the limitations of its scope more definite. Writing or signing a contract, however, should not be forced on members; they must agree that a written statement is preferable to one that is spoken. A spoken contract has the advantage of flexibility—something that may be desirable for a particular group. Some task groups (e.g., committees) use written minutes to record the group's actions and then briefly review the minutes at the beginning of the next meeting as a check of their accuracy. Because the previous meeting's content and process presumably are based on the group's contract, approval of the minutes is tantamount to a verification of the contract by the group. In groups with open membership (see Chapter 1), the group must renegotiate its contract at every meeting. Finally, whether or not the group's membership changes, it is likely that the group itself will change as it develops over time (or fails to develop): The contract, or some portions of it, will need to be reviewed and perhaps renegotiated throughout the entire life of the group. Do you believe that the Contract Negotiation process you described was handled effectively? Why do you think so?

_____

_____

_____

HOW DO YOU KNOW
THAT YOU HAVE NEGOTIATED
A SUCCESSFUL CONTRACT?

There are several indicators that a contract has been negotiated successfully, including such things as: members come to the meeting at the agreed-upon time; they use their own words to describe the terms of the contract in a way that everyone else in the group thinks is correct; they help to work out the ways in which the group operates and then follow these procedures; they stick to the topics they agreed to pursue; they help one another to find answers to problems, for example, when the problem of a member comes to the group's attention, they suggest different ways of handling it instead of criticizing him or her for having such a problem; and so on.

OPPRESSION AND EMPOWERMENT
IN RELATION TO CONTRACT NEGOTIATIONS

The purpose of Contract Negotiation is to achieve a consensus of members and leader(s) about the roles and goals of their group. This means deciding what the group is about and how it will operate. To some degree, this is determined by the nature of the group's sponsoring organization. A psychiatric hospital is not likely to set up support groups for people with multiple sclerosis. But a psychiatric hospital might create a support group for its ex-patients, with a major purpose being to help these individuals remain in the community with no need for rehospitalization. Ex-patients of psychiatric hospitals, however, are one of the oppressed populations that experience discrimination when, for example, they go job hunting. Given that reality, it could certainly be appropriate to include attention in the group's contract to issues pertaining to negative labeling in general and dealing with job discrimination in particular. It would also be appropriate to include planning for and carrying out social activities in the group's contract, both for sheer enjoyment of members who have known depressed states and to enhance social skills that are essential to healthy social functioning.

Suppose Company X is hiring low-skilled persons, but members of the ex-patient support group report that X is discriminating against them because of their hospitalization backgrounds. The group has to consider whether or not it wants to take on the risky business of confronting this discrimination and working to empower its members when, for example, they encounter prejudice in a job interview. If you are that group's Leader, you need to decide with the members how realistic it is to build empowerment-enhancing activities into the contract.

In other words, the process of Contract Negotiation can be used to help a group consider what its priorities should be with regard to oppression and empowerment. But a group is not bound to its original contract. Helen Northen (1955) wrote about a group of African-American adolescent women who started out as a social club meeting in the local YWCA. They planned several very satisfying activities, but when they tried to plan a trip to a nearby roller-skating rink, they were turned down because of their race. The members met, renegotiated their contract, and began a campaign to break the color barrier based on their new contract.

Moral: When dealing with a group composed of individuals who are identified as members of one of the oppressed groups discussed in Chapter 1, it is very likely that you want to address issues of oppression and empowerment in the group's contract.

AN EXAMPLE OF CONTRACT NEGOTIATIONS

SCENE

The Center is an experimental day treatment program for young adolescents who have demonstrated severe emotional difficulties, leading, in most cases, to expulsion from public school. Twelve boys and girls, ages 11 to 14, spend five days a week, from 8:45 a.m. to 2:30 p.m., at the Center. The program is a federally funded research-oriented program that is studying better ways of helping such disturbed (and disturbing) children. The children are all of average or better intelligence; none are psychotic. Prior problematic behaviors include uncontrolled rages, temper tantrums, assaultiveness, refusal to attend school, withdrawal from peer contacts, and generalized depression.

This particular example of Contract Negotiation focuses on the staff's attempt to handle one problematic situation, rather than on an attempt to negotiate a contract with the entire group in relation to the agency's overall program. Specifically, several of the children have been slipping away from the Center's building to steal candy and soft drinks from either a local market or the gas station on the corner. Staff members have decided that it would not work to tell the children that this cannot be tolerated because such a statement would only serve as an invitation to test the staff's ability to control their behavior. Instead, it was decided to propose that the children and staff together develop their own candy store, in the building, using a standard cooperative mode of operation.

Each morning, when the children arrive, there is a meeting in the group worker's room to discuss plans for the day and any issues that may arise. The term *meeting* is used loosely—the children usually are not able to sustain any discussion without pushing each other, jousting verbally with the staff, and disrupting any orderly discussion. Based on prior experiences, this particular meeting went pretty well for this group, considering the difficulties they have had with joint problem solving.

Staff members include:

Joe: The group worker
Dan: The teacher
Tony: The arts and crafts specialist

Children include:

Rich: Fairly new but already physically dominant in the group
Mary: Recently deposed by Rich but still feared by the other children; tough and very bright; the group's only black member
Dave: Already Rich's willing lieutenant
Don: An angry loner
Sara: Large for her age, occasionally teams up with Mary
John: Disliked because he steals from others in the group
Billy: Silly, hard to get close to
Frank: Easily defeated, cries easily, often a scapegoat
Mike: Loud-mouthed bully easily terrified by more aggressive children

Jane: Pasty-faced, overweight, jointly despised by Mary and Sara

Barb: Newest child in this program, refused to attend school and must be compelled to come to the Center

(Keith: The smallest and most easily terrified child, stayed at home because of a bad cold.)

ACTION	DISCUSSION
JOE: OK, I guess you all know that Keith has a bad cold and won't be here.	Joe hopes that members will, in time, come to care about one another.
MARY: Who cares.	Members make it clear that they do not care. In fact, they make similar negative comments when any of the other children do not attend, as if to say, "Who needs anyone?"
RICH: The little jerk!	
DON: Who needs the creep?	
JOE: Just thought you'd like to know. Listen, we've got a serious problem we want to talk about with all of you.	Joe decides to move quickly to the major issue, knowing the low tolerance for serious discussion in this group. He tries to get their attention by adopting a serious, worried tone, rather than by chastising them.
MIKE: Big deal!	
TONY: Seriously, Mike. Listen to Joe.	Tony supports Joe's attempt to begin Contract Negotiations.
MIKE: Aw—!!	
JOE: Well, here it is. We know that some of you have been visiting the little market down the street and the gas station, without permission, to rip off candy and soda. We've got to do something about it. Not only is it wrong, if the people at either of the places call the police and	Joe presents the problem: no accusation, just a statement of known fact. And he tries to make clear that the staff's primary concern is the welfare of the children.

they catch you, you'll be in big trouble, and I'd hate to see that happen.

MIKE: Big deal!

Mike wants the spotlight.

Rich: Shut up, big mouth! You already said that. So what are you big deals gonna' do about it? Lock us up?

Rich has to prove he is top dog. He wants to know what the staff is going to do, guessing that it will be punishment.

DAN: Cool it a minute, Rich, and listen to Joe. He's got a proposition to make you guys.

Dan makes it clear that Joe is acting as spokesperson for the staff and tries to gently control Rich.

SARA: Joe is going to make us a proposition? Tch, tch—what would your wife say?

A different form of provocative testing.

JOE: Probably that I better watch my step. No, really you guys. This could be big trouble for you. But we have an idea that you might like, and here it is. If what you want is candy and pop—stuff like that—why not make our own store here, run it ourselves, put the kind of stuff we want in it, then sell it to ourselves?

Joe tries a light response, then moves on quickly to the idea for a store. He begins to state the goals of the contract, get a Center-based candy store into operation run by staff and students together.

DAVE: Sell it to ourselves?

Dave, at least, is interested.

JOE: Yeah, what I mean is—well, it's called a co-op. That's short for "cooperative." See, each of us puts up some money for a share of stock. That means you own a piece of the store. We take all of that money and buy candy and stuff at a wholesale place—just like the market does, but when we buy it from our store, we charge the same prices the market does.

Joe begins to describe the role of stockholder, hinting at other roles that they would play in relation to the store.

RICH: That's dumb, knothead. If we can get it so cheap, why should we pay as much as you have to pay at the market?

Rich doesn't understand the proposal. He just knows he doesn't like it.

MARY: Yeah, and you clowns wouldn't let us get what we wanted anyway.

Mary seems interested in Joe's idea but is already beginning to set conditions for her participation.

JOE: I don't see why not, Mary, providing it's not booze or something weird like that. And look, Rich, lots of other people come to the center, like Connie, Rita, and the other women.[1] And from time to time, we have other visitors who want to see how we run this place—university students and folks like that. They could buy stuff from the store but the profit would only go to the stockholders at the end of the year. *You* and us—we would be the stockholders so the profit would be divided among all of us, and just us.

Joe tries to get the idea across that control of the store would be shared, further clarifying roles. He tries again to ignore the edge in her question through humor. He then answers Rich's questions without responding to the name calling. In the process, he tries to clarify further the way in which the store would operate. Also, he shows that he can work with Rich and the others without asserting his power as an adult.

DON: Hey, Tony, you gonna' open the shop? I wanna' work on my mosaic.

Don is feeling anxious—too much talk. In addition, he probably does not understand the idea yet.

BILLY: Too much talk! Too much talk! Squawk, squawk! Polly want a cracker! Awk!

Billy, too, is feeling uneasy and latches onto Don's wish to end all the talk.

TONY: Look, I guess it's hard to put up with all this talk, but try, will ya'? Let's see if we can get this worked out. Then I'll open the shop, Don.

Tony tries to show that he understands their discomfort but appeals to them to try to stick with the negotiations a bit longer.

MARY: Yeah, shut up, Billy. Well, who will run it . . . you guys?

Mary is still suspicious and pushes for greater role clarity.

JOE: Well, we thought that would be up to the stockholders—you guys and us too—but we hoped you'd run your own store, and, of course, we'd help. See, in a co-op, the only people who get to vote and the only ones who get the profit are people who buy stock.

JOHN: And how much would the stock cost?

JOE: Good question, John. It would be up to all of you to decide. What do you think would be fair, John?

JOHN: I dunno.

MIKE: Ten dollars!

MARY: Ten dollars? Shoot! Just what I'd expect from you, dummy. I don't have that kind of money.

BILLY: Ten cents! Ten cents! That make sense.

JOE: Well, Billy, I guess everyone could get that but—uh—12 kids, 3 staff—that's 15 of us, times 10—that's $1.50. Couldn't

Joe makes it clear that control rests with stockholders—children and staff—further clarifying their role. Both voting and monetary profit can be seen as a payoff for accepting the contract that Joe is proposing. And they will get the candy and pop that they want without risk (although the risks involved in stealing may actually have been a major payoff for them—that remains to be seen).

John, quiet until now, asks a practical question—apparently he has been listening.

Joe rewards John for asking a problem-focused question that moves the negotiation forward. He tries to make clear that such decisions are up to the group by throwing it back to John.

John does not feel strong enough in the group to risk a suggestion.

A bit of showing off from Mike.

Mary puts him in his place and thus proves to her own satisfaction that in spite of Rich's ascent to power, she is still powerful in the group. But her blast at Mike covers a real concern about her own limited financial resources.

Billy tries to make a contribution that involves a play on words.

Joe treats Billy's suggestion as a valid contribution, albeit not financially realistic.

buy much candy with that, could
you?

MARY: How about $2.00
apiece. That's—lessee—that's—
ummm—12 of us and 3 of you—
that's $30.00.

Joe thinks, "Mary's hooked!
And she's smart enough to help
us over some rough spots."

RICH: Well, I don't like it, and
I ain't gonna' buy no stock.

Rich is not as quick to understand the co-op idea as Mary,
but he is smart enough to see
that he may not be able to control this idea because of the "majority rules" procedures involved.

MARY: Forget you! Who needs
your lousy money! Without him
we'd still have—uh—$28.00!

Mary has not forgotten that
Rich recently deposed her. Perhaps she sees the store as both
a good idea in itself and a way
of regaining her position of top
dog in the group.

Before this discussion ended, the figure of $2.00 a share was agreed
upon. They decided that everyone would bring their $2.00 the next day,
although Rich held out. (A week later he gave in when, with the store
a reality, he realized that he had absolutely no way to control it, because
he was not a stockholder and could not vote on any store-related issues.)
They also decided that the group would make up a list of desirable
candy and—with money in hand—Joe and Mary would purchase the
store's candy from a local wholesaler on behalf of the group. Don and Billy
became interested in building a counter and locked cabinet for the store's
supply of candy and asked Tony to help them do this in the shop. The
contract for the co-op store appeared to have gotten off to a good start.

EXERCISE

Goal

When participating in a group you should be able to help negotiate
an agreement (with the other members) that leads to a consensus on
goals and roles that members will play, as well as specifying "criteria"
and "payoff" for this contract. *Note that you will need a tape recorder
to record this discussion.*

The tape recording you are about to make is to be used later for an exercise in the chapter on Gatekeeping, so be sure to save it. Although an audiotape recorder is acceptable, a videotape recorder might be even better. One of the best ways to practice Contract Negotiation is to negotiate a contract for your own group. As you have probably learned by now, members of your group are participating in it for a variety of reasons. If the way you work together as a group is to be efficient and useful, a contract is a necessity. In addition, you can learn a great deal about group participation techniques through the experiences you share in the development of your group as a group. The contract provides a way of highlighting aspects of group interaction so that you can be aware of some of the development achievements and difficulties faced by any group.

Follow the format proposed in the previous discussion of Contract Negotiation. One reminder: The write-up suggests that contracts often have to be renegotiated at a later date. You may want to revise yours as well, later on. Whatever you do in your discussion, be sure to work out an agreement to the following question:

Where in the scheduling of future sessions should the chapter on Starting come? Originally, it was placed as the last technique to be presented, with the idea that you might be starting a group after completing this book. However, agency staff members who field tested the earlier version of this book, *Participant's Handbook Group Leadership Techniques* (1972), indicated that a better plan might be to start working in or leading a group *while participating* in this group, so that you can use this group for support and consultation purposes. If you do that, the chapter on Starting may well be directly applicable to your work now or soon, and you will not want it to read it last. If you decide to leave Starting until the end, you could agree to continue meeting as a group, even after you have completed this group, to provide each other with support and help in relation to your new group(s).

POSTSCRIPT: CONTRACT NEGOTIATION

An underlying assumption of the preceding discussion on the contract is that democratic processes (e.g., majority rules, etc.) are always best. Given the wide diversity of group types and purposes, however, it is certainly relevant to at least challenge that position.

In a series of classic experiments studying the differential effects of authoritarian, democratic, and laissez-faire styles of leadership (Lewin, Lippitt, & White, 1939; White & Lippitt, 1960, 1968), members preferred the democratic leaders to the other two varieties, but when the autocratic leader was present, members (boys, ages 10 and 11) "worked hard, demanded little attention, only rarely engaged in horseplay, and closely followed his recommendations. Apparently, the relationship between participation and effectiveness is not a simple one" (Forsyth, 1990, p. 242). Stogdill (1974) reviewed more than 40 studies dealing with leadership styles. He found some studies indicating group productivity *decreased* when group members participated in decisions, but the majority of studies found no differences resulting from the centralization of decision making. Satisfaction with the group was highest under democratic leadership, but not when the group expected the leader to act in an autocratic fashion (Foa, 1957) or when the group was very large (Vroom & Mann, 1960).

In general, researchers have found that no single leadership method is best in all situations. Although it seems best to me to involve members in decision making when a major decision is to be made, it may at times prove dissatisfying if it is ineffective and time consuming for members. In such a situation, centralized decision making may work better. Although more research needs to be done on this subject, I would suggest that whatever processes are used within the group will be used to greatest effect if all members are involved in contract negotiations that designate when and how group decisions are to be made.

IN PREPARATION

For the Rewarding exercise, you will need a collection of pennies, peanuts, or some other small objects (that people would probably like to have) to give away. Check the description of the exercise to determine the number of objects you will need. It would help to have a timing device available as well.

NOTE

1. Joe is referring to program volunteers who spend one day a week at the center.

SUGGESTED READINGS

Barker, R. (1986). Spelling out the rules and goals: The written worker-client contract. *Journal of Independent Social Work, 1*(2), 67-77.

Benianti, J. (1989). Pilot project for male batterers. *Social Work With Groups, 12*(2), 63-74.

Corder, B., Haizlip, T., Whiteside, R., & Vogel, M. (1980). Pre-therapy training for adolescents in group psychotherapy: Contracts, guidelines, and pre-therapy preparation. *Adolescence, 15*(59), 699-706.

Croxton, T. (1974). The therapeutic contract in social treatment. In P. Glasser, R. Sarri, & R. Vinter (Eds.), *Individual change through small groups* (pp. 169-186). New York: Free Press.

Croxton, T. (1988). Caveats on contract. *Social Work, 33*(2), 169-171.

Greene, G. (1989). Using the written contract for evaluating and enhancing practice effectiveness. *Journal of Independent Social Work, 4*(2), 135-155.

Ingram, R. (1992). When therapy is oppression. *Transactional Analysis Journal, 22*(2), 95-100.

Participant's handbook group leadership techniques. (1972). Ann Arbor, MI: Manpower Science Services.

Rose, S. (1989). *Working with adults in groups: Integrating cognitive-behavioral and small group strategies.* San Francisco: Jossey-Bass.

Specht, H. (1986). Social work assessment: Route to clienthood: II. *Social Casework, 67*(10), 587-593.

Wilcoxon, S. (1990). Developing consultation contracts: Applying foundational principles to critical issues. *Journal of Independent Social Work, 4*(3), 17-28.

Chapter 5

REWARDING

HOW DO YOU DESCRIBE REWARDING?

Rewarding is any action that tells a group participant or a group as a whole, "You've done something effective in moving toward an individual or group goal." Its intended result is to encourage the individual or group to continue and/or increase the frequency/intensity of particular goal-directed behaviors.

People often tend to confuse the terms *rewarding* and *reinforcement*. *Reinforcement* is the process by which the performance of some act is *continued or increased due to some stimulus that directly follows the act* (i.e., responds to the act). To distinguish between Rewarding and reinforcement, think of Rewarding as a *conscious* effort to continue or increase the occurrence of certain acts that, in this instance, pertain to the goals in either the group's contract or the individual's contract with the group. Reinforcement therefore, is a *result* and occurs as a chain of events in which an individual (or a group of individuals) behaves in a particular way, is rewarded for *that* behavior, and then continues or increases the intensity of the behavior so that the probability of that behavior occurring in the future can be said to have been enhanced, or "reinforced." So, for example, Tim, a quiet member, speaks up, others praise (reward) him for his contribution, and he begins to speak more often during group meetings. But an individual's behavior can be reinforced *even though no one intended to reward that behavior*. For example, when some members disrupt problem solving by clowning around, other members who give a lot of attention to the clowning behavior may inadvertently reward the clowning (assuming that the

clowning member finds attention from others to be rewarding) without meaning to reinforce it. *Rewarding, then, is an attempt to achieve reinforcement of behaviors that are viewed by the rewarding person as constructively relevant to the contract.*[1]
What is an example of Rewarding in a group that you have experienced?

_____

_____

_____

WHEN DO YOU REWARD?

If you have made a contract with one or more group participants to help change a particular behavior and that behavior does change, you follow through on the contract by rewarding that new behavior.

A group member who has responded to criticism by getting angry says that she would like to control her temper, and you (as Leader or as member) have agreed to help her. Later in the group meeting, this member is criticized for one of her opinions but remains calmer than she usually does when criticized. Because you and she have agreed that behaving in that way is one of the goals she is working toward, you reward her by praising both her self control and the productive way in which she carried on the discussion despite the personal criticism.

When you make such an agreement, you reward a member every time he or she more or less meets the agreement. As time goes by, you can raise your expectations so that rewards are only given for *better* performance. And when the agreed-upon level has been reached, the performance of the individual only needs to be rewarded from time to time to *maintain* the level of performance. The danger of *not* Rewarding every time in the beginning of an individual's attempt to acquire a new way of behaving is that the rewarder may forget to reward at all, even occasionally, and the person then may feel ignored or may not realize that you are still pleased by his or her behavior. You should keep good records or notes of group meetings to make sure that you have not stopped Rewarding. Eventually, you *can* plan to cease Rewarding altogether when the individual is, in effect, clearly Rewarding himself or herself for the behavior (i.e., if he or she stopped to think about it, the person might think, "Hey! I did that right! Good for me!").

You use Rewarding when a member behaves in a way that you would like to see in the future, even though you have made no specific contract about that behavior.

When a member asks the group for help in handling some situation that is difficult for him, he has done two things that should be rewarded. First, he has recognized a difficulty and admitted it (or described a task that they need to accomplish). Because this is a step toward longer-term goals, it does represent progress. Second, he has done something about this difficulty by asking for help. Assuming that you want to encourage both behaviors, you would reward him (for example, by giving the requested help or by getting the group to give help and support).

You reward a member *in the presence of other group participants* when he or she has handled a situation in a way that you would like the *others* to imitate. This increases the possibility that others will view this person as a role model and will imitate that member.

In the early stages of a group's development, members tend to be polite to each other and not say what they really think because they do not want to get into disagreements. There is often so much emphasis on superficial togetherness and good feeling that no one wants to say or do anything that would appear to contradict it. Then a controversial topic arises and one member expresses some mild disagreement with the opinions of others. You praise that member for expressing a point of view. Others in the group will see the member's behavior as a model for them to imitate. Your public praise has let them know that giving their own opinions is an expected and desirable action in the group. (More on this later, in the chapter on Modeling.)

In the example of Rewarding that you described, was it used at the appropriate time? Why do you think so?

_____

_____

_____

HOW DO YOU REWARD?

Find out what would be a meaningful reward (or payoff) to a person. A *reward* is something someone likes to do or wants to have. A colleague or someone you supervise might have a favorite task at work;

when you give opportunities to do that task more and some less enjoyable task less, you are Rewarding him or her. For most people, paying attention to them (Attending) and showing interest in what they are saying and doing is a meaningful reward. You find out what is rewarding by asking directly or by observing what pleases them. For example, you observe what they do during their free time or how they relax after accomplishing some difficult or complicated task.

Once you know what they consider a reward, review your resources to make sure that you have or can find a way to reward them as they would like to be rewarded. (Make sure that the reward is socially and legally appropriate, as well.)

When the goal is to achieve change in a member's behavior, you should negotiate a contract concerning the particular behavior(s) that will be rewarded. Ask the participant to describe these behaviors in his or her own words to make sure that you both mean the same thing. Observe the member's behavior so you know when he or she behaves correctly and deserves his or her reward. Then reward the individual *as soon as possible after he or she behaves in the agreed-upon way*, unless the giving of a reward would in itself disrupt the behavior that you want to have continued. In that case, reward later, but in either case *make sure that the person being rewarded is told that the reward is for a particular behavior.*

A group member who wanted to work on her difficulties with people concentrates most of her talk on complaints about the unfairness of others. Finally, she tells of a way that she handled someone's teasing—a way that she recognizes as ineffective. The Leader wants her to continue describing her response and says, "Thanks for telling us about what *you* do when someone hassles you like that. That's great!"

Attention Is Rewarding. We often pay attention to ineffective or self-defeating behavior and, without meaning to do so, we reward such behavior. This has the effect of encouraging behavior that should not be continued. Try to ignore behavior that should not be continued, while Rewarding only behavior that appears likely to move an individual or the group toward previously defined goals. It is helpful to make a distinction between behavior that you do not like but can tolerate because it does not interfere with the group's progress or the members' goals and behavior that should not continue because it is harmful for the group or for the goals of the person who is behaving that way. The first kind of behavior should simply be ignored or handled neutrally— neither rewarded nor punished. Behavior that should not continue could also be ignored but later commented on as a violation of the contract, along with praise for more contract-related behavior.

A male member of the committee made cutting remarks repeatedly about the new chairperson, who happened to be a woman. His most irritating comments dealt with the fact that, as a woman, she could not run a meeting very well. The chairwoman gave as good as she got. The result was a steady increase over time in his taunting statements, which had the effect of interfering with the discussion of important issues. After a while, she realized what was going on and ignored the teasing while noting the positive contributions the member had made as the committee's senior member. In time, his teasing of her during meetings diminished and his comments about her took on a more friendly quality.

You can help people get closer to an effective way of doing something by rewarding initially for any behavior that resembles the desired behavior to some degree, and then Rewarding only those behaviors that come closer to the behavior you want to achieve.

Early on, you might reward talking in general just to get the group going. Later, you would reward talking about the agreed-upon subject. Finally, you would reward specific kinds of talk about the subject—talk that helps the members of the group reach goals associated with the contract.

When giving someone feedback about his or her attempt to learn a new way of behaving, *first* reward those portions of the behavior that are correct, *then* tell the member which portions, if any, need correction or further practice.

During a role play in which one member attempted to imitate another's demonstration (in an earlier role play) of how to ask a teacher for help, the group worker praised her for her fine imitation, and then suggested a few additional words she might say.

Refer to your example of Rewarding. Was the technique used effectively? Why do you think so?

_____

_____

_____

HOW DO YOU KNOW
YOU ARE REWARDING SUCCESSFULLY?

You know you are rewarding successfully when the member(s) continue to act in the desired or agreed-upon way—a way that you intended to reward. The members may behave only partially that way, but the change is recognizable. Or, they begin to use the behavior as part of their normal pattern, incorporating it into their lifestyle.

A member comes to the group meeting on time more often than in the past; group members offer each other suggestions in more helpful ways; there is increased interaction among group members, with less talk directed to the Leader alone; and so on.

Successful rewarding also results in the member(s) continuing to behave according to the agreement you have made. Even if the behavior satisfies only part of the agreement, the rewards have worked if the number of correct behaviors grow or if the members' behavior more closely approximates the agreed-upon goals.

When you reward *without an agreement* (e.g., you praise a member when he or she makes constructive comments about other members), you are likely to find that the rewarded behavior increases relatively slowly, with frequent occurrence of the wrong behavior (such as harshly criticizing other members). But when rewards are used with a clear agreement, the new behavior often begins at once and continues with only rare backsliding. In other words, Rewarding with a contract achieves its goals faster. Be careful not to take the new behavior for granted too soon or stop Rewarding before the member has found his or her own rewards (including his or her own self-esteem) to substitute for the ones you have been providing.

In the example of the candy store created with the youngsters in the Day Treatment Center (see Chapter 4), members brought their $2.00 for their share of stock and were praised by Joe for following through on their agreement.

Another way to know that you are rewarding successfully is when other members use the rewarded behavior as a model and imitate this behavior at appropriate times. Check to see whether the others are increasing their performance of particular behavior(s); for example, when you have praised a member for giving his or her own point of view, do the others simply increase their amount of talking as if they thought you were praising talk in general, or do they increase the behavior you praised, thus expressing their own point of view?

Members begin to express different points of view openly within the group in imitation of the member you rewarded for going beyond surface agreement. If the members seem to have missed the point of the praise—that is, if they talk more, but do not really express their own points of view—reward the talk in general. Then remind the group that the member you praised gave his or her own opinions and that is good. Focus your rewards on the particular kind of talk that will move the group forward.

OPPRESSION AND EMPOWERMENT IN RELATION TO REWARDING

The attempt to use a reward to enhance group interaction implies that the Leader has sufficient control of meaningful rewards to distribute them for "reward-worthy" behavior. It also implies that the Leader *knows* which reward will work best for which particular client population. A lonely and depressed child, for example, may find attention rewarding. But an adolescent from a discriminated minority group may have good reason to be suspicious of a smiling adult group Leader who uses praise to reinforce a particular behavior that occurs during a group meeting. How then do you select rewards that help shape behavior? Who should have control of the distribution of these rewards?

Assume that you are trying to help an individual become empowered in her or his attempts to change the behavior of other individuals or of a large system or organization. The adage that "nothing succeeds like success" would seem to apply here. Winning a local civil rights battle could be very rewarding. Short of actually achieving complete success, praise of an individual's attempts to learn and implement a change strategy (where the individual is helped to recognize that the praise is relevant to the strategy he or she is trying to develop) could also be a powerful reward. It would also help if members were encouraged to create a norm of rewarding one another with praise and verbal encouragement when it is clear that a member is working hard on individual and/or group goal achievement. The important thing is that the member is helped to recognize the link between his or her behavior and some desirable outcome that pertains to empowerment, and to feel that he or she deserves the reward, so that he or she does not see it as an attempt to create conformity and behavior designed primarily to make the group worker comfortable.

AN EXAMPLE OF REWARDING

The School Lunch Committee of the city-wide Parent Teachers Organization (PTO) Council is meeting at the home of Mary, its chairperson. Members (each of whom represents the PTO Board of a local elementary school) are Michele, John, Henry, and Bob (Bob is also Vice President of the council). The group's purpose is to draft proposals for development of a hot-lunch program for the elementary schools. Currently, children can bring sack lunches, but the school only provides milk. The committee was created in response to complaints about the lack of a hot-lunch program, as well as concerns that the program was being poorly run—with inconsistent discipline, food being thrown around, dirty eating facilities, and so on. Early on, the group decided that they needed a sense of the community's opinions with regard to the hot-lunch program, so they developed and circulated, with the help of the school administration, a survey questionnaire to parents of the 9,000 elementary school children in the district. The purpose of this meeting was to begin the task of evaluating responses to the questionnaires.

ACTION	*DISCUSSION*
MARY: [At the door greeting John, the last to arrive]. Hi, John! Good to see you. Now we're all here and on time!	Mary rewards John for simply arriving, and on time.
BOB: If that's meant for me, touché! But after you promised to bake your famous strawberry cheesecake if I made it on time—well, how could I resist? Hi, John. Try this cheesecake. Absolutely fantastic! Mary, you sure could teach a lot of people how to start a meeting on time.	Based on a contract to reduce his late arrival behavior and replace it with on-time arrivals. Bob was on time and did get his reward. Bob now rewards Mary with praise of her culinary skills. Obviously, he would like to see Mary and others bring refreshment (especially cheesecake) to future meetings.
HENRY: I second the motion, and since we're all here, could we start? As hungry as I was for Mary's delicious cheesecake (Is there enough for seconds?), I also want to find out what we found out.	Henry also rewards Mary. Good feelings all around, setting a positive tone for the meeting.

MARY: Help yourself, Henry.
Well, here's the computer print-
out. There's a lot of data here, but
as I read it, we may be in for
some surprises.

Rewards the group for gathering
by having the computer printouts ready for them.

JOHN: How do you mean?

MARY: Well, this is just a superficial opinion because we really
need to study the data and do
some cross-tabs, but anyway, it
seems to me that some folks in
some schools are pretty satisfied, while in some other
schools, they're pretty dissatis-
fied. I mean, the problem may
not be as system-wide as we
thought. Anyway, I summarized
some of the data on these sheets.
Here's one for each of you.

The two rewards for participating on this committee are to be
given information that is interesting and to get that data before
anyone else in the community
has it.

Another reward by a well-
prepared chairperson.

HENRY: It's great the way you
got this stuff out of the computer so
quickly. Let's see. How many people sent their questionnaires back?

Henry, on behalf of the committee, rewards Mary's activity in
preparing everything on time.

MARY: Thirty-seven percent. See
the figures? Right there on the
summary sheet? Thirty-seven percent isn't bad, wouldn't you say,
Michele?

Michele has not spoken so far.
In an effort to draw her in (so
she can be Rewarded for participation), Mary addresses a question to her.

MICHELE: Well, considering
we used the kids to take it home
and bring it back and didn't try
to follow up on no-responders,
I'd say it's a very good response.
Most of the school bulletins my
Stanley is supposed to bring
home arrive crumpled and un-
readable, if they arrive at all. It's
interesting though: According to
this data, we did get a better re-

sponse rate in some schools than in others, and at first glance it appears that there's more discontent in schools located in the lower socioeconomic areas of town.

BOB: Hey, you know you're right. I hadn't seen that. I was trying to link up school size and satisfaction. But it seems to have more to do with geography and SES. Sharp eyes, Michele.

MICHELE: Thank you kindly, Mr. Vice President.

JOHN: SES?

HENRY: Socioeconomic status.

JOHN: Oh yeah, I see. Well, Michele, you've got a better sense of where each school is located and the SES of that area than I have.

HENRY: OK, seems to me that if we look this over and answer some questions like that one, we'd be ready to go to the Board of Education and work on them to make some changes.

BOB: Whoa! Not so fast. I'm not sure that we really know what the data says. And besides, once we've figured that out, we still have to go back to PTO Council with it.

Bob rewards both Michele's participation and her ability to make sense of complex data. He lets her know he is rewarding her ability to analyze data, but his Attending response to her statement also serves to reward the simple fact of her participation.

Michele rewards the rewarder. This could lead to more complimentary remarks among members in general.

Attending is Rewarding. Henry attends to John's questions.

Again Michele is rewarded by a group member for the knowledge she shared with the group.

Disagreements are important for a group's development. Henry is pushing, and Bob is openly disagreeing. At this point, Henry is violating the group's contract and Bob is telling him so. In doing so, he may be, in effect, Rewarding Henry's participation but certainly is not trying to reward him for forgetting to report first to the PTO Council.

HENRY: Oh, no! If we do that we'll never get any action! The Council reps will each have to take it back to their own PTO Boards and—why, it will take forever! Can't we short-circuit that?

BOB: I don't see how. After all, we're just a committee doing some legwork for the council.

MARY: Well, look, Henry, maybe what we've got to do now is set up a schedule for analyzing the data, especially the open-ended questions—the computer didn't handle those—and then work out some plan through Bob to get our report before Council so we can move on this, maybe in time for this year's school board elections. I'm with Henry—I don't want this to take forever, but if we jump the gun, we might alienate Council. And without its backing we don't stand a chance with the school board.

HENRY: Yeah, well, I guess you're right, Mary. I always want to go off half-cocked. I get so damned impatient with committees! OK, let's set up a schedule, like you said.

MARY: OK, but I'm glad you raised the point. It gives us all a chance to see where we are. And don't worry about going off half-cocked. We're not here just to agree on everything. Now, let's begin to figure out the dates for our schedule.

Henry increases the intensity of his participation. It is apparent that he trusts the group enough to disagree with some of its members.

Mary steps in to mediate the disagreement. In doing so, she is careful to make a distinction between Henry's introduction of a disagreement with the group's original contract and her own support for the original contract, partially because it's not up to them to change it at this point. She supports Henry's right to his position and, in a sense, rewards him for verbalizing his impatience. Here she could be said to reward the act of disagreeing without accepting the content of that disagreement.

Henry rewards her mediating behavior. He recognizes the need to abide by the contract. It is hoped that he will continue to voice his disagreements.

Mary makes sure it is clear she rewards Henry for openly expressing his views and that she hopes he will continue to do so. In other words, he should know why she rewarded him.

The committee then worked out a schedule for analyzing the findings, preparing a report based on their analysis, circulating it to PTO Council members, and presenting the report at a monthly meeting of Council.

EXERCISE

Goal

When participating in a group meeting, each member of the group will be able to use Rewarding so that other members (if asked) (a) would report that they were being rewarded, (b) could report why they were being rewarded, and (c) could describe the way in which the reward pertained to the goals of the group's contract and do so correctly, in the opinion of the Rewarder. In addition, it's quite acceptable to have fun doing this exercise!

Time Required

Number of members multiplied by five, plus 15 minutes. If this is a fairly large group, you might select a group of six members and seat them in a small circle inside a larger circle formed by the rest of the group.

Materials

Container of pennies, peanuts in the shell, wrapped small candies, or other small objects, which the participants are likely to view as valuable or fun, to be used as rewards. Multiply the number of members by 50 for the maximum number of rewards you will need, and you should have more than enough. Obviously, the reward you use will depend on who is in the group and the resources that are available to you. It should be made clear to everyone before you begin that once the exercise is ended, members may keep the rewards they have been given.

Specialized Roles

Members take turns being Rewarder. When playing this role, they hold the container of rewards and distribute them any way they wish. It is recognized that having only one Rewarder operative in the group at any one time is a bit artificial in that, in real life, anyone in a group can reward anyone else at any time (or use any of the other techniques described in this book, for that matter). In this sense, the exercise is not designed to simulate reality as much as it is designed to have you experience the responsibility of Rewarding when you are formally given the power to do so. In addition, you will need one "minute-taker" and one "time-keeper," although the group's Leader (if you have one) might take on one or both of these roles.

Process

In this exercise, the group will design a way of evaluating the effectiveness of this book (or, if part of a larger course, *this* portion of the course). While working on this assignment, members take turns distributing rewards to the other members with regard to their contribution to the successful completion of this task. Because you will be creating a procedure that could actually be used, a person to take minutes is needed so that the ideas generated in the discussion can be recorded. To make sure the minute-taker does not miss a turn as Rewarder one of the other members should be asked to take the minutes during the period when the minute-taker has a turn as Rewarder.

It will help if the group uses a timer to limit each member's time in the role of Rewarder so that everyone has an equal turn in that role.

When everyone has had a turn, the round is ended. If the group task has not been solved to the members' satisfaction, the discussion may continue, as time allows, *after* the group has discussed its reactions to the Rewarding aspects of the discussion. If the discussion is then continued, the group may wish to continue the Rewarding process in order to put into practice the insights they have gained from their review of their own Rewarding behavior.

Concluding the Exercise

After the exercise is over, discuss your experiences. Cover such questions as: (a) Was appropriate behavior rewarded? (b) Was it rewarded at the right time? (c) Did the Rewarding succeed in improving the performance of individual members and of the group as a whole? (d) Was any behavior reinforced that the Rewarder did not intend to reward? In every case, relate the discussion of your experience to the kind of group with which the group members are familiar. (Occasionally groups using this exercise have added "punishment" by taking away what was earlier given as a reward. It certainly makes for a more lively experience! Consider adding that to this exercise.)

POSTSCRIPT: ISSUES IN REWARDING

The subject of Rewarding has received a great deal of attention in cognitive-behavior modification literature (see, for example, Rose, 1989). In thinking about this whole area, you may want to ask yourself the following questions:

- What does it feel like to get rewards?
- What does it feel like *not* to get a reward when you believe you have done something effective or productive? Is it the same as feeling ignored? Rejected?
- How does receiving or not receiving expected rewards affect your attitudes toward and perceptions of the Rewarder or of other group members who did receive rewards?
- What are Rewarders trying to communicate about themselves when they give out rewards? Are some of them trying to look like "good guys" who are generous to others? Does that help them reward effectively, as far as the criteria of contributing to the group plan or cohesiveness is concerned?
- Are some Rewarders you know quite stingy in their distribution of rewards? What are the implications of such stinginess for the use of Rewarding?
- Have you found that the recipients of rewards usually understand why they are being rewarded?
- How does it feel to be a Rewarder and to have to decide who deserves a reward? What do you do about those feelings? How does that affect your rewarding behavior and your feelings about your responsibilities toward other members?
- Do you find that you have a tendency to give more rewards to those behaviors that were active and highly visible compared with those behaviors of a more subtle nature, such as attending, smiling, and leaning forward in interest?
- How did your personal opinion of someone giving a reward affect how you felt while being rewarded?

Although group time may not allow a thorough discussion of all of these questions, you will find it useful to reflect on them as they relate to your own experiences. Then ask yourself, How do my answers to these questions relate to my work with clients, contacts with fellow staff members, interactions with other students and/or professors, participation as a committee member, and so on?

NOTE

1. When attempting to change behaviors in the direction of *reducing* or *eliminating* some behavior(s), it is essential to *replace* the unwanted behavior with something else. For example, if you want someone to *stop* shouting, you need to be clear about the fact that you want the person to start speaking in a reasonably modulated tone of voice instead.

SUGGESTED READINGS

Anstey, M. (1982). Scapegoating in groups: Some theoretical perspectives and a case record of intervention. *Social Work With Groups, 5*(3), 51-63.

Emurian, H., Emurian, C., & Brady, J. (1985). Positive and negative reinforcement effects on behavior in a three-person microsociety. *Journal on the Experimental Analysis of Behavior, 44*(2), 157-174.

Fagot, B. (1985). Beyond the reinforcement principle: Another step toward understanding sex role development. *Developmental Psychology, 21*(6), 1097-1104.

Gill, S., Menlo, A., & Keel, L. (1984). Antecedents to member participation with small groups: A review of theory and research. *Journal for Specialists in Group Work, 9*(2), 68-76.

Porterfield, J., Blunden, R., & Blewitt, E. (1980). Improving environments for profoundly handicapped adults: Using prompts and social attention to maintain high group engagement. *Behavior Modification, 4*(2), 225-241.

Sharpley, C. (1982). The effects of age, group-size, and classroom social homogeneity upon the extinctive properties of implicit reward conditions. *Alberta Journal of Educational Research, 28*(4), 301-314.

Waltzer, F. (1984). Using a behavioral group approach with chronic truants. *Social Work in Education, 6*(3), 193-200.

Chapter 6

RESPONDING TO FEELINGS

HOW DO YOU DESCRIBE
RESPONDING TO FEELINGS?

Empathy is the ability to *sense* how people feel about something. *Responding to Feelings* refers to the action—verbal or nonverbal—by which we communicate empathic understanding; that is, what has been sensed about people's feelings. Thus in a group, one can sense and discuss emotions that are being felt by one or more members; for example, "Sounds like you're upset that John didn't do what he had promised to do."

This is an important aspect of group participation. Social workers know that clients are unlikely to become involved in a trusting way with anyone who ignores or is insensitive to their feelings. But feelings are equally important in work with task groups. For example, members of a committee who feel ignored or rejected are not very likely to feel loyal to, and work hard for, the committee if other members make them feel that way.

What is an example of Responding to Feelings in a group that you have seen recently?

_____

_____

_____

HOW DO YOU RESPOND TO FEELINGS?

You can Respond to Feelings of others in three ways:

Make a mental note of the feeling but decide to make no response to it at that time and go on with the discussion.

Indicate that you recognize and understand the feeling by saying so, then proceed with the discussion.

Stop the discussion and focus on the feeling or the issue that caused it.

You can attempt to work on the emotion so that the person (a) has it under control, (b) has explored it enough so that he or she can focus on what can be done about the things that cause the emotion, and/or (c) has resolved the issue. Then continue the discussion.

The three options are discussed in the "When Do You Respond to Feelings?" section. For now, it is important to know how to (a) recognize a feeling, (b) respond to the feeling, and (c) confirm the accuracy of your response.

Recognizing the Feelings

The first step is to recognize the feeling components of whatever is going on. Attending is required—not only to what is being said but also to how it is being said in terms of tone of voice, rapidity of speech, emphasis on particular words, and body language (i.e., facial expression, body posture, hand gestures, etc.) present. Tune in to the feeling component, not the cognitive content alone. The feelings can sometimes be quite different from what the words say. For example, a member says, "It's OK with me," but tone of voice and facial expression display resentment. It is also useful to attend to yourself and how you feel; your feelings may serve as clues to what is going on in others. For example, if you are feeling vaguely anxious, you should ask yourself if you are feeling anxious because one (or more) of the group's members is (are) generating a strong feeling. If so, you have recognized that they may be feeling angry. Perhaps you are feeling anxious in response to the same thing that is making them anxious; your feelings are a clue to how they are feeling. In this case, you have used your feelings to recognize theirs. Perhaps you are feeling defensive. Is someone attacking you indirectly or expecting or demanding something that you cannot deliver?

Describing the Feelings to Yourself

The second step is to put the feelings into words—at least to yourself—so that you can label or identify them correctly. There are several ways to do that: You can compare the feelings you have recognized in others with similar feelings you have had; that often suggests the words for the feelings. You also can compare the current feelings with feelings you have experienced in the past, then recall what brought them on.

Confirming Your Description of the Feeling by Responding to Feelings

The third step is to check the accuracy of your observation and description with the individuals you are trying to understand.[1] Responding to Feelings—sometimes called "verbal empathic responding" (Milnes & Bertcher, 1975)—seems to work best when you:

1. Begin your statement tentatively, thus allowing for correction by the other person; for example, "I get the feeling that . . .", "Sounds like . . .", or "I wonder if you are saying that . . .".
2. Make specific reference to the feeling, trying to select the word or phrase that most accurately reflects the feeling you are trying to describe. Here, the choice of words is very important if you want to reflect the individual's feelings accurately. For example, there are subtle but important differences between each of the following "feeling" words: furious, angry, annoyed, and peeved. Your problem is to *select* the word or words that *best* describe(s) the feeling and, at the same time, the word(s) that communicate(s) best in the language of the person(s) to whom you are talking (e.g., "pissed" may be far better than "angry" when speaking to a particular individual).
3. Relate the feeling to something, someone, or some situation; for example, "It seems to me that you've been feeling very lonely *ever since your friend moved away.*"

In regard to your example of Responding to Feelings, was it used effectively? Why do you think so?

_____

_____

_____

WHEN DO YOU RESPOND TO FEELINGS?

Deciding when, and if, to respond to feelings depends, in part, on the purpose of the group. Discussion of feelings may be the prime purpose of some groups, but in other groups, solving a particular problem (such as how to write a policy statement on which everyone can agree) may be more important. In the latter case, the emphasis is on deciding what the members can do to make the situation come out right, not on their feelings about the policy. Nevertheless, as committee members work on a policy statement, strong feelings are often expressed—feelings that should not be ignored.

Some occasions when you only make a mental note are:

- When identification of the feelings would embarrass the individual by calling attention to the underlying message in his or her behavior; for example, when the person is pretending to be uninvolved but really is not.
- When the group has a full agenda and appears able to finish the agenda on the contracted schedule only if it avoids dealing with the feelings of some of its members—especially if the feelings are intense, and attention to the feelings would interfere with the group's schedule.
- When you (or another group member) have become so emotional about something that it would throw the group off topic if members got involved in an emotional exchange—especially if the topic is important and the feeling issue irrelevant to it.
- When you think that the group is not able to respond to the emotions of one member and is likely either to withdraw from interaction or engage in off-topic conversation in order to avoid these emotions.

Add to the list from your own experience with different kinds of groups.

_____

_____

_____

Some occasions when you simply acknowledge feelings are:

- When a member's words or actions give evidence of an emotion that she or he seems ready and willing to share with the group or that has been recognized by the group.
- When it is not possible to ignore feelings without seeming dumb, disinterested, or phony. If the group task does not require resolution of those

feelings, you could say something like, "It seems to me that you're worried about how this situation will turn out. I guess there's not much we can do except wait and see what happens and hope that it goes OK. In the meantime, we might as well continue to . . .".

- When there seems to be a general mood of the group that you cannot put your finger on, as if they are reacting to something you do not know about. You could say something like, "Things seem strange in here today. I get the feeling that we're all (upset, annoyed, preoccupied, nervous, etc.). What seems to be going on? Anybody have any ideas?" Or, "Could somebody tell us how she or he is feeling right now?".

- When the feelings are too strong or too apparent to be overlooked but are about something that is out of range of the group's business (although the contract could be renegotiated to include the problem), or about an event that the group cannot undo (e.g., a death in a member's family), or is so limited to a particular individual, and with so little relevance to the group's business, that it can be handled better outside the group, even though the group has to acknowledge its awareness of the emotion.

Add to the list from your own experience with different kinds of groups.

_____

_____

_____

Some occasions when you discuss the feeling or the issue that caused that feeling are:

- When someone has given evidence of important feelings, and you believe that discussion of the feeling will facilitate group progress toward its contracted goals.
- When the group progress will be blocked until the feeling or the issue is brought out and resolved.
- When the group's goal involves the feelings of members, for example, helping members develop ways of dealing with fears of entering new situations.

Add to the list from your own experience with different kinds of groups.

_____

_____

_____

In regard to the example of Responding to Feelings that you described, was it used at the appropriate time? Why do you think so?

_____

_____

_____

HOW DO YOU KNOW
THAT YOU HAVE RESPONDED
TO FEELINGS CORRECTLY?

When you make a mental note only:

- Individuals feel free to discuss their feelings when they are ready to do so, instead of hiding them, because they have confidence that they will not be compelled to discuss those feelings that they prefer to keep to themselves.
- The tasks on the agenda are completed pretty much as scheduled.
- Group interaction continues around the contracted issues, and the atmosphere of the group is comparatively comfortable.
- The group continues to work together, and the persons whose feelings you have noted maintain their level of participation.

When you acknowledge a feeling:

- The individual verifies that you have understood the feelings correctly by agreeing with you or by subsequent behavior (e.g., the apparent relief at getting something off his or her chest and being understood or by moving on from expressing the feelings to deciding what to do about them).
- The discussion continues and remains relevant to the contract.

When you discuss the feeling or the issue that caused it:

- The group will participate in a focused discussion of the feeling or the issue behind it, work it through, feel more "whole," and show an increase in mutual supportiveness, like people who have survived an emotional experience together. Thus there also should be an increase in good group behaviors such as Attending, Information Giving, and Rewarding.

OPPRESSION AND EMPOWERMENT
IN RELATION TO RESPONDING TO FEELINGS

Verbalizing empathy as a response to a client's expression of feelings is designed to encourage that client to trust the group worker and the group itself as a major step in the helping process. But what about the observed fact that some people are less likely to express (verbally or nonverbally) *any* feelings in public than other people are? For example, in one woman's support group, a member described a very unpleasant incident with her mother, and the group worker commented on the fact that the other members' response was surprisingly bland. One of the members then explained that she had trained herself to hide her feelings; in her family, if you showed that you were upset about anything, everyone teased, prodded, and poked until the victim left the table in tears.

If one works on the assumption that members who hide feelings are avoiding involvement in the helping process, then it makes sense to look for ways of creating an atmosphere of comfort in which the open expression of feelings can occur. This may require considerable sensitivity as to the meaning of a public expression of feelings for a particular population. Thus one may have to be patient with a group of men who avoid feelings. Or one may need to study the cultural backgrounds of clients to learn how, when, and if it is seen as appropriate to deal with feelings in front of others.

In some groups, however, the issue of feelings takes on a very different slant, and these are the groups whose members have experienced oppression and are very angry about it. In my own experience as a group worker, for example, I have seen a great deal of rage acted out through violence and rule-breaking behavior. This violence can be frightening for the group worker, who may be afraid that the inability to control such behavior can lead to someone getting hurt—including the worker. In these cases, the goal is to help the individuals **talk** out, rather than **act** out, their strong feelings so that, eventually, they can begin doing something constructive to change the circumstances (such as racial prejudice) that they find so infuriating. Nevertheless, it's important for it to be legitimate to express such negative feelings—indeed it seems essential if these individuals are going to make appropriate and effective use of their group experience.

AN EXAMPLE OF RESPONDING TO FEELING

SCENE

The New Horizons Club is a social club for adults who have been patients in a psychiatric hospital. Sponsored by the local mental health association, it is a small part-time program, employing a social worker, Sue, 10 hours a week. The group meets in a modest three-room apartment on the third floor of the United Fund Building, a small three-floor building in downtown Metropole. The apartment is open three evenings a week from 7 p.m. to 10 p.m. Tonight the meeting will include a planning session to finalize plans for a trip to a local bowling alley. Eight members are present.

Jim: President, the official "opener" and "closer" of the club's apartment; slow of speech, easily rattled, he has been a club member longer than anyone else. Jim lives with a hospital staff member who is his legal guardian.

Dorothy: Also a long-time member who lives at home with her husband. Sharp tongued, she tends to misuse confrontation, driving sensitive individuals away.

Min: White-haired, straight talking, works in a nursing home. Was hospitalized for 30 years because, "I saw things that wasn't there," she says.

Rita: 30, obese, unkempt, shy, little affect.

Sadie: Loud-speaking, insensitive to the way she overwhelms others.

Jerry: Tall, soft-spoken veteran, says little, attends regularly but is nevertheless a fringe member.

Rae and Esther: A couple who met at the club, now living together; she has two small children who also live with them. Rae, a veteran, has had severe drinking problems but has good social skills and is outgoing.

People have drifted into the living room and an informal meeting has begun.

ACTION	DISCUSSION
SUE: So, Rae, Esther tells me you've got a bowling alley all lined up for us?	Sue, the group's social worker, gives Rae a chance to shine for the good advance work he did on behalf of the club.
RAE: Yeah, well—yeah. Star Lanes, over on Anderson Street. They said they could handle all	Rae is a comparatively new member.

of us—you know—we said we'd take those folks from the nursing home, too—all of us—up to 20— a week from Wednesday evening, 7:30 to 9:30, and they'll knock 10 cents a frame off the price.

JIM: I hope ya' didn't make the reservation, yet. I'm—I'm not sure I wanna' go. B-bowling's no f-f-fun.

Jim's negativism may be because Rae has assumed power too quickly for Jim. Sue makes a mental note to pay particular attention to the threat Rae may pose to Jim's feeling of importance, gained from being President. On the other hand, something else may be bothering Jim. It is too early to know just what his feelings are.

SADIE: Oh, Jim, cut the crap! You'll love it!

Sadie misses what appears to be Jim's feeling that his position is threatened.

DOROTHY: Well, I can't bowl. I've tried it. And besides, Rae shouldn't have made reservations without asking us first! Rita, you don't want to go, do you?

Jim's negative reaction causes Dorothy to verbalize her concerns—she cannot bowl, and Rae acted with too much authority.

Sue listens, trying to sense what is troubling members who had said last week that they would like very much to go bowling. Dorothy appears to want support.

RITA: Well . . .

Rita does not know what to say.

RAE: Hey, wait a minute! Bowling wasn't my idea. I just said I'd look into it for the Club. What's going on here?

Now Rae feels put upon. He put himself out for the Club, and besides, the plans are still tentative. He is getting mad and, in another minute or two, may tell Jim and Dorothy to go to hell and walk out.

SUE: Sounds like you're pissed that nobody appreciates what you did on behalf of the Club.

Sue senses his frustration and responds to that feeling. Still she wants to know more about Jim and Dorothy's feelings and waits before responding to them. Also, she wants to focus on Rae's feelings without appearing to accuse the other members of double-crossing Rae, which might happen if she said, "It must be frustrating to have the members ask you to do something and then back out of it—even bawling you out for what you did."

RAE: Yeah. OK, that's right.

Rae recognizes he has been understood and calms down a bit.

DOROTHY: Well, I didn't ask you! Besides I always feel silly when my ball rolls in the gutter.

Dorothy persists, which is typical of her.

MIN: Makes you feel damned silly, don't it—I mean not hittin' anythin'.

Min responds to Dorothy's feelings of ineptitude, thus providing support for Dorothy's right to feel inept and demonstrating empathy for some of Dorothy's feelings.

DOROTHY: That's right. And last time we went bowling—all those people starin' at us like we wuz freaks or somethin' . . .

Dorothy lets Min know that she understood, and then adds another concern, perhaps the most important: that people will know she has been in a psychiatric hospital when they see her with these "crazy-looking" club members.

SUE: You mean it makes you uncomfortable 'cause people look at you as if you're peculiar.

Sue senses that this is really what is troubling Dorothy and decides to check it out with her.

DOROTHY: That's it exactly. It's like they know we were in the hospital.

Apparently a bull's-eye! The "ball in the gutter" talk was only a cover-up for her underlying concerns.

RITA: You're right. Just like my landlady always lookin' funny at me. And the other day I woke up at 10 in the morning. I didn't want anyone staring at me, so I pulled the covers up over my head and stayed in bed.

This starts a new train of associations for Rita. Sue has touched a responsive chord in Rita who is also troubled about the way people look at her as an ex-patient. Sue is thinking, "This is important for Rita, but first the group as a whole should decide about the bowling trip." She decides to suggest proposing an additional item to the group's contract to be dealt with later: how to become more comfortable in new social situations.

SADIE: Might still be there if I hadn't called you up, huh, dearie? See I called her 'cause sometimes she gets down. So I been callin' her every morning.

Sadie is looking for praise because she helped Rita, away from the group, when Rita was feeling depressed.

SUE: Sadie, it's great that you cared enough to call her up. And Rita, it must be rough feeling that it does not matter to anyone whether or not you get out of bed. I guess Sadie understands that. Well, we need to talk about that. But maybe we should get back to this bowling trip and talk about whether or not we go, OK? [Pause—Rita nods her agreement.] Seems to me some people feel very uncertain about it—even though last week we did say we were interested in bowling—because they think they'll be embarrassed by low scores and by people staring at us. So I wonder if that's what's really troubling some of you; going out in public as a group?

Sue rewards Sadie for help she has given Rita and lets Rita know she understands Rita's feelings of despair, but asks her to hold this topic for a bit so they can decide about bowling.

Sue tries to state what she senses is the group's ambivalence and feelings about this public activity away from the safety of the club room.

DOROTHY: Well, maybe that's it. 'Cause I've gone bowling with my husband and—well—when I go with him I don't bowl good, but it's still OK.

Dorothy confirms that Sue is on the right track as far as she is concerned.

As the discussion continued, Sue attempted to help the members share their feelings about public reaction to their appearance and what they might do about it. She knew that the general grooming of the members left much to be desired; many of them did look peculiar, inadvertently calling attention to themselves. Later, she returned to Rita's problem of sleeping late each day. Tucked away in her mind was a decision to pay attention to the possibility that Jim felt threatened by Rae's assertiveness. In addition, she hoped that her rewarding of Sadie's sensitivity to Rita's depressed feelings would lead other members to become more empathic to one another.

EXERCISE

Goals

When participating in a group, you should be able to recognize feelings of the members and describe them to the members in such a way that members would confirm, if asked, that you have described their feelings correctly.

Time Required

45-60 minutes

Materials

None

Specialized Roles

One member at a time plays the role of presenter, the others play the role of responder or observer.

Process

Divide the group into subgroups of three

In each subgroup, one member (the presenter) should tell the responder (for 5 minutes) how he or she feels about one of his or her roles in life (e.g., student, spouse, worker, parent, etc.) that is important to him or her. The responder should try to respond verbally and nonverbally—through facial expression, bodily posture, and so on—to the feelings being expressed as they are expressed (i.e., do not wait until the end of the 5 minutes). The responder should capture the feelings as completely as possible with all the subtle shades of meaning involved. The responder may be tempted to move to problem-solving responses of Information Seeking or Information Giving, but should resist the temptation in favor of responding to feelings that are expressed, implied, or sensed throughout the 5-minute period because this is an exercise in Responding to Feelings, not a realistic attempt to solve a problem. One person in the subgroup should act as observer, to both observe and watch the time. After the first 5 minutes, all three should review the preceding 5-minute exchange. The presenter should describe his or her reactions when the responder hit the nail on the head or when the responder was off the mark. The observer may point out behaviors that the presenter and responder may not have been aware of, the accuracy with which the observer thinks the responder identified the presenter's feelings, the impact of the responder's statements on the presenter and vice versa, and so forth.

After 5 to 10 minutes of discussion, rotate the three roles—with a new presenter, responder, and observer—and repeat the above process. Repeat the process until everyone has had a chance to perform in all three of the specialized roles.

Next, if time allows, reconvene the larger group and discuss the insights and observations made during the exercise. The following questions could be discussed:

- Were feelings correctly identified? If not, why not?
- What were the reactions of the presenters to the responses made to them?
- Were the responders aware of their own emotional responses? Did the observers think the presenters were always right in judging whether the responders were on or off target in identifying the presenter's feelings?
- What kinds of positions did presenters choose to discuss and why? What feelings about self, family, and society were involved in people's feelings about the positions they chose? Did feelings about the positions they chose have some effect on the way they felt about themselves, others, and society, or was it that feelings about these things (self, others, society) determined how people felt about their positions?

POSTSCRIPT:
ISSUES IN RESPONDING TO FEELING

There are two feelings that are often overlooked that play an important role in group participation. When these feelings are overlooked, there are negative results for the group. The first feeling is that one's participation will be rejected by the group, so it is better to play it safe and just listen. The other feeling has to do with the disappointment associated with an attempt to participate that is generally ignored.

As a teacher, I have dealt with feelings of threat associated with active participation in a variety of ways. Subgrouping seems to help—students will say things to one another (e.g., in groups of two) that they will not say to the larger class. Having said what they said in the subgroup, it's easier to "report" on this exchange to the class. Dramatic activities, such as role playing or watching a videotape or film, also help to unlock cautious participation. Likewise, small group exercises (such as those in this book) help. It's important to reward participation when it's relevant to the group's contract, as in the chapter on Gatekeeping. But it is also important to recognize members' feelings of apprehension about participation, to plan for it, and—following the rules made explicit above—to comment on the apprehension if and when it interferes with group participation.

The other feeling (being ignored) can lead members to withdraw and lower their participation. I saw this happen in a course in which students were subdivided, by interest, in small project groups. In one group, a very verbal, very bright member had, without realizing it, come to dominate all group participation. The other members (there were two) had given up trying to make any significant inputs and were simply going along with the talkative member. But one of them commented on it to me. It was my custom to meet with every project group from time to time, and when I met with their group and observed the dominant member in action, I spoke with the three of them about this. I commented to the two that it might be difficult to be part of a group in which their input seemed not to be valued. They agreed and initiated a discussion that led the third member to recognize the impact of her over-participation on the other two members. Fortunately, she recognized the importance of reducing her activity, and the group moved on to a greater equality in the division of talk time.

Unfortunately, this sort of resolution often does not occur because the feelings about being ignored go unrecognized. Perhaps this post script will alert you, the reader, to the problem so you can act on it, if and when it occurs.

IN PREPARATION

You will need a 5-by-8 card folded lengthwise (so it can stand on a table) with the word "Focuser" (written with a dark thick felt pen) on both standing sides of the card.

NOTE

1. Obviously you do not check it out during the meeting if you have decided to make a mental note. After the meeting, you can check it out with the person; for example, "I had the feeling that you were sore at me today."

SUGGESTED READINGS

Batson, C. (1991). *The altruism question: Toward a more social psychological answer.* Hillsdale, NJ: Lawrence Erlbaum.

Bennett, C., Legon, J., & Zilberfein, F. (1990). Empathy in clinical social work. *Clinical Social Work Journal, 18*(1), 57-72.

Berger, D. (1987). *Clinical empathy.* Northvale, NJ: Aronson.

Gladstein, G. (1987). *Empathy and counseling: Explorations in theory and research.* New York: Springer-Verlag.

Goldstein, A., & Michaels, G. (1985). *Empathy: Development, training and consequences.* Hillsdale, NJ: Lawrence Erlbaum.

Jackson, E. (1986). Behavior in groups as a predictor of internal empathy and communication empathy. *Social Work With Groups, 10*(1), 3-16.

Kissman, K. (1992). Parent skills training: Expanding school-based services for adolescent mothers. *Research on Social Work Practice, 2*(2), 161-171.

MacKay, R., Hughes, J., & Carver, E. (Eds.). (1990). *Empathy in the helping relationship.* New York: Springer.

MacKey, R., & Sheingold, A. (1990). Thinking empathically: The video laboratory as an integrative resource. *Clinical Social Work Journal, 18*(4), 423-432.

Manor, O. (1986). The preliminary interview in social group work: Finding the spiral steps. *Social Work With Groups, 9*(2), 21-39.

Marquilies, A. (1989). *The empathic imagination.* New York: Norton.

Pinderhughes, E. (1984). Teaching empathy: Ethnicity, race and power at the cross-cultural treatment interview. *American Journal of Social Psychiatry, 4*(1), 5-12.

Raines, J. (1990). Empathy in clinical social work. *Clinical Social Work Journal, 18*(1), 57-72.

Williams, C. (1989). Empathy and burnout in male and female helping professionals. *Research in Nursing and Health, 12*(3) 169-178.

Wortman, J. (1990). Empathy and social work: The capacity of students for cognitive and emotional empathy as it relates to field instruction evaluations. *Dissertation Abstracts International, 51*(4A), 1392-1393.

FOCUSING

HOW DO YOU DESCRIBE FOCUSING?

Focusing means calling the group's attention to something that has been said or that has happened to (a) highlight or clarify it so that the group will be more aware of what has occurred or (b) bring the discussion back to the agreed-upon business of the group.

What is an example of Focusing that you have seen recently?

_____

_____

_____

WHEN DO YOU USE FOCUSING?

1. When a contribution that could move the group toward its goals is over-looked by the other members; for example, they do not use good questions, suggestions, or pieces of information because the contribution comes from someone with low status in the group, was said too quietly, or was said in an unclear way.

2. When the discussion shifts, without any agreement to shift, from the group's topic and continues off-topic for several minutes, without any attempt to return to the original topic.

Sometimes you find yourself having to use Focusing repeatedly in one meeting. When this happens, you should ask yourself why the group is continually straying off the topic. Perhaps the topic is producing too much anxiety. Perhaps it is of little interest to most members. Perhaps the group thinks the Leader wants to change the topic. Or perhaps there is another issue that members really want to discuss, thus requiring renegotiation of the contract. When that happens, Focusing is used to call the group's attention to their continual drift from the subject. This would be an instance of Focusing to draw the attention of the group to its inability, over time, to stick to the topics it had originally chosen.

In regard to your example of Focusing, was it used at the appropriate time? Why do you think so?

_____

_____

_____

_____

HOW DO YOU FOCUS?

If a Leader thinks that Focusing is needed, he or she should first wait to see if members of the group will perform this function.[1] After a few minutes, if no one uses Focusing, the Leader should look for an opening to politely (but firmly) call the attention of group members to whatever it is he or she wishes to highlight. The Leader may have to insist that the group attend to his or her Focusing behavior. As an example, suppose the group has been talking about ways to explain a police record to a prospective employer. Pete thinks honesty might be the best policy. This gets John going on a lengthy tirade about "pigs who always get down on black people." A Leader might then use Focusing as follows: "John, the way in which police behave toward black people is very important, I agree, but talking about it right now won't help Pete on his next job interview. Why don't we get back to that, and then, if you still want to, we can talk about the police."

If you use Focusing to draw the group's attention to a contribution that has been ignored because it was misunderstood or not heard, it often helps to clarify the contribution by rephrasing it into words that are commonly understood in the group, or by asking the person who made the contribution to restate it so everyone can hear it. If you rephrase what has been said, make sure that the original speaker thinks you have interpreted his or her point correctly.

When people are always going off the topic—either because something else has come up that they feel is more important or because the current topic is not as important as the group thought it was when the contract was negotiated—renegotiate the contract to add the new topic. You can agree to take up the new topic at once, or you can ask the group to schedule it for later, after the agreed-upon topics have been covered. But, in general, a group will go nowhere if it follows every passing interest and whim.

In the example of Focusing that you have described, was its use effective? Why?

_____

_____

_____

HOW DO YOU KNOW
YOU HAVE FOCUSED PROPERLY?

1. Members consider an on-topic contribution that was previously ignored. Further, their response results in increased participation by the contributor.

2. If the group has strayed from the agreed-upon topic, it either returns to that topic or agrees that the new topic is of more immediate importance. If the group stays with the new topic, it must agree on some way of handling the original topic, such as to drop it entirely, take it up at a later time, return to it after they dealt with the new topic, or make a tie-in from the original topic to the new one.

3. Members will address the problem of continually drifting off topic (if this occurs), analyze the cause, set up some ways of resolving the difficulty, and continue with the business of the group. Because the need for continual Focusing may indicate that the group has only a fuzzy idea about a contract they thought was explicit, the resolution of this problem may very well involve a renegotiation of the contract itself (see Contract Negotiation).

OPPRESSION AND EMPOWERMENT
IN RELATION TO FOCUSING

Earlier, I noted that Focusing is sometimes used when the group begins to drift from its agenda. This drifting can occur when a member forgets about, or is made uncomfortable by, a particular issue. A simple reminder from the group worker may be enough to refocus the group on its original topic. But when the group drifts more than once, you can suspect that at least several members—if not the group as a whole—are not comfortable with what is going on, and they want to get away from it. As the group worker, you have to ask yourself, Just what *is* going on? Say the group members and group worker are from different racial, ethnic, or gender groups (this is often the case). It is possible that the members are uncomfortable with the group worker's failure to understand some issue that pertains to the various kinds of discrimination they face outside of the group. Even more difficult, the group worker may have said or done something that members find offensive, and they are not ready or willing to confront him or her about it. Under such circumstances, it is understandable that members would find it difficult to stay focused on the agenda.

So, for example, a white worker working with a group of clients, all of whom are black, might need to ask: "Does the members' inability to stay focused on a previously group-selected topic grow out of their concern about my unintended, yet unfortunately, offensive words or actions?" When you suspect that this may be occurring, it may be necessary to stop the group's activities and gently ask with no hint of annoyance or defensiveness, why the group is having so much difficulty with this particular topic. This should elicit a response that encourages an open discussion of what is troubling the group. When this happens, it heightens the group worker's understanding of the impact of his or her behavior on the group, and it increases the worker's awareness of what these members find offensive. As group workers, we must always be open to this kind of learning, even though it can be uncomfortable. In the long run, openness to this kind of learning can only serve to enhance openness of communication within the group.

AN EXAMPLE OF FOCUSING

The John Smith Home is a residential treatment facility for emotionally disturbed boys and girls between the ages of 6 and 14. The institution has a capacity for 35 children living in five separate cottages. The administrative staff of the Home (all social workers) consists of a director, assistant director (who supervises the houseparents), group worker (who supervises a full-time assistant, David, and six part-time recreation workers, all male), director of social services, and a caseworker (these last two each carry half of the child population as their caseload). The administrative staff meets weekly for 2 hours to review a range of administrative issues. In addition, they meet whenever a crisis situation warrants some joint problem solving and decision making. The action that follows depicts such a meeting: Mrs. Grey, an experienced and highly competent child-care worker, has just learned of her mother's unexpected death in another part of the country. Mrs. Grey's family situation is complicated by her father's illness. Now that his wife is gone, he will probably have to be institutionalized. Mrs. Grey has to leave today and estimates it will take at least 2 weeks and maybe a month to settle her mother's estate, see to her father's needs, and sell their house. There is no available replacement, and, to complicate matters, her cottage has just received a new girl (Mary Beth) who has already caused considerable turmoil.

Jane: Director for the past 12 years, is responsible for having changed the institution from custodial care to the status of a well-regarded treatment facility.

Jim: Assistant Director, 4 years on the job, a solid administrator, well-liked by all.

Max: Group Worker, joined the staff 3 months ago, straight out of a master's program in a school of social work.

Ruth: Social Service Director, 6 years at the agency; started as caseworker and was promoted when the former Social Services Director resigned. Extremely competent, well-organized.

Bart: Caseworker, 3 years at the agency; was a classmate of Ruth's in a school of social work. Warm; good with children.

ACTION	DISCUSSION
JANE: I suppose you all know about Mrs. Grey?	
MAX: I heard that her mother died unexpectedly and that puts her in a bind about her dad. And that she's leaving today. How long is she going to be gone?	Max is very task focused.
JIM: At least 2 weeks, maybe more.	
BART: How are we going to cover for her? Oh boy, this couldn't come at a worse time.	Here is the question the group must answer: Who will be in charge of her cottage during the day until she returns.
JANE: Why?	

BART: With Mary Beth in the cottage—well, she's been raising 10 kinds of hell over there, and Grey thought she might be getting somewhere—at least there was a beginning—but now—oh brother! Damn!

Bart makes it clear that it will be particularly difficult to substitute for Mrs. Grey at this time because of the presence of a newly placed child who has been upsetting the cottage routine.

RUTH: Well, but what's Mrs. Grey's situation?

Ruth, ever compassionate, is concerned about Mrs. Grey.

JANE: Well, her folks lived in the same house for more than 40 years. And last year her father had a stroke that left him pretty helpless. The mother was handling it okay but—well—now that she's gone, there's no one to take care of him.

By answering in some detail, Jane allows the group to wander from the prime issue: replacing Mrs. Grey until she can return. As the Leader of this group, Jane is not, at this time, maintaining an appropriate focus on the group's primary goal.

MAX: That's rough. [Pause] I wonder if we could move Mrs. Garcia into her position until she returns.

Max, still task focused, suggests one solution. However, as the group's newest member he is more or less ignored.

JANE: Well, possibly.

RUTH: Does Mrs. Grey have any other options? Like, are there other family members who could help?

Ruth is, for the moment, more concerned with Mrs. Grey's problems than with the administrative issues of cottage management.

JANE: Apparently not. And to make it worse, she's got to deal with a housing developer who's been wanting to buy the house so he can tear it down and put up some new apartments. And it seems there's something in the will that might mess that up.

Jane continues off-topic, in an almost gossipy way.

RUTH: I wonder if she could contact Legal Aid about that.

And now the group is off to the races thinking about Mrs. Grey's problems.

BART: Why Legal Aid? She may have a lawyer of her own.

JANE: No, she doesn't. I already asked her.

JIM: Well, you know, I think it's fine that we're worried about Mrs. Grey. But aren't you overlooking the most important thing? I mean what do we do about her cottage while she's gone? Now Max had one suggestion that kind of got lost.

Jim, whose job is to run the day-to-day operations of the home, uses Focusing to get the group back on target. He also calls attention to Max's suggestion.

RUTH: Sorry, Jim—I'm just feeling so badly for Mrs. Grey.

JIM: No sweat, I'm worried about her too.

MAX: I just said maybe we could move Mrs. Garcia in to take Mrs. Grey's place while she's away. She gets along with that group. Took over in the cottage last weekend and seemed to do OK. Even seems to like Mary Beth, but don't ask me why. She's hell on wheels!

Max now presents a suggestion for coping with Mrs. Grey's absence, their original reason for meeting; move Mrs. Garcia, a newly employed child-care worker, into the cottage to fill Mrs. Grey's position while she is away.

JANE: Yes, Mrs. Garcia might be good. Although she is pretty green.

Jane now attends to Max's suggestion and voices a concern as to its feasibility.

BART: Well, she's new with us, but she did have 2 years of experience with that group foster home back East.

JANE: Well—not speaking against Mrs. Garcia, but I have my doubts.

RUTH: Gee, what if Mrs. Grey's situation won't let her come back at all?

Ruth introduces another side issue, albeit one that is clearly related to the major issue.

JANE: We'll cross that bridge if and when. And if we move Garcia, we'll have to figure how to cover for her. Now let's see. Is there any other way we could manage the coverage in Grey's cottage?

Jane maintains the group's focus by placing that question in its proper perspective, then invites further suggestions about the group's primary concern.

The group continued with its discussion, finally deciding to move Mrs. Garcia to Mrs. Grey's cottage and contacting a former child-care worker to cover Mrs. Garcia's responsibilities on a temporary basis. This woman had recently returned to the community, and Jim had heard she might be looking for part-time work. He telephoned her and found that she was definitely interested. She agreed to come by later that afternoon to discuss details.

EXERCISE

Goal

When participating in a group meeting, you should be able to recognize when the group drifts off topic and use Focusing to get the group back on topic, or agree to modify the contract to deal with the other issue.

Time Required

About 40 minutes: 24 minutes for problem solving and 16 minutes for review of the experience

Materials

A 5-by-8 card folded lengthwise with the word "Focuser" written with a thick felt-tip pen or dark crayon on both sides of the card

Specialized Roles

Members of the group will work to solve the "Same-Same" problem described below. (If anyone by chance has run into this problem in the past and knows the solution, he or she should be an observer.)

Process

The group will be given a problem to solve. (The problem is of the brainteaser variety and has a logical solution.) Members are to take turns placing the Focuser card in front of them and then move it around the group to each member in turn at about 4-minute intervals. When the Focuser sign is in front of a member, he or she should make a particular effort to use Focusing to help the group solve the problem. However, any member can use Focusing whether or not the card is in front of him or her. The group must try to solve the problem before everyone has completed one turn as Focuser.

THE SAME-SAME PROBLEM

There once was an island called Same-Same, in which all of the inhabitants looked alike. On this island, two religious sects had developed side by side: Members of one were called (translating from the original) Truth-Tellers; members of the other were called (again, translation) Liars. As their names imply, Truth-Tellers *always* told the truth; Liars *always* lied.

A famous anthropologist decided to study these diverse side-by-side cultures. She was warned that her task would be impossible because all of the islanders looked alike, regardless of whether they were Truth-Tellers or Liars.

She arrived in a small boat, buffeted by a pounding surf. She gasped when she saw three men approaching: They did, in fact, all look alike! The roaring of the surf drowned out the first man's words, spoken when he was still about 50 feet away. He was pointing to himself, as if to introduce himself, and smiling in a friendly way.

Inviting her to join them, she and the little group moved away from the pounding surf. When he could make himself heard, the second man said, pointing to the first man, "He said he was a Truth-Teller." The third man said, "Don't believe him (pointing to the second), they're both Liars! I'm a Truth-Teller." The famous anthropologist smiled. She knew which was which, and why. Do you?[2]

In discussing the exercise, you might pay particular attention to any of the following questions:

- What factors led the group to attend to some member's contribution and overlook or fail to recognize the value of contributions from others? Status? Friendships? Assumed or demonstrated expertise? Language styles? Something else?
- What factors affected the effectiveness of Focusing attempts?
- Were there times when Focusing should have been used but was not? How did this affect the problem-solving process?
- How does Focusing pertain to the other techniques that have been covered so far?

POSTSCRIPT:
ISSUES IN FOCUSING

As I have thought and written about these techniques, it has become clear to me that each is connected in some way to the others. As a way of concentrating on this thought, here are some ways that Focusing links with each of the other techniques.

Attending. Focusing can be used to prepare members for future issues or events, by drawing attention to the fact that they are coming up soon. Announcing a meeting agenda when a meeting begins is a simple example: It focuses members' attention on the order of events in today's meeting so that they are ready (and Attending) when items come up.

Information Giving. You focus the group's attention on something by giving relevant information about it, either as a way of introducing something or making sure everyone has the necessary information to deal with it.

Information Seeking. One way to focus the group's attention on a subject is to find out what members already know about it. Encouraging members to query each other draws the group's attention to that subject. It also helps to focus on what further information, if any, is needed.

Contract Negotiation. A major function of the contracting process is to give the group a sense of purpose—that is, a *focus*—so that members can concentrate their energies on the matters that are of importance to the group, rather than wandering all over the map.

Responding to Feeling. Some groups appear to operate on the principle that working on tasks to accomplish goals is the group's primary function. This point of view overlooks the very important role that feelings play in any group's life. It is often necessary to use Focusing to help a group pay attention to "feeling" issues that are being overlooked because, practically speaking, inattention to feelings is one of the prime impediments to the development of group cohesion.

Rewarding. When a particular member has made a contribution to the group's progress toward its goals, Focusing can be used to draw the group's attention to that member's activity, thus Rewarding his or her good work.

Summarizing. The purpose of Summarizing is to focus the group's attention on what it has accomplished so far in relation to the goals it negotiated in its contract. Summarizing also focuses the group on what it needs to do next.

Gatekeeping. Focusing on quiet members, to draw them in, and on over-active members, so they will allow others to contribute, is essential to achieving the balance of participation that is associated with the success of any group—success in terms of *both* goal achievement and widespread member satisfaction with, and attraction to, the group.

Confrontation. Sometimes it is necessary to firmly inform a member, a subgroup, or the group as a whole that there is an inconsistency between their words or actions and the goals of the group, or the norms by which the group has agreed to operate. This kind of Focusing is called Confrontation.

Modeling. We use Modeling to help one or more members learn *about* and learn *how* to do something. But to be effective, a model has to be noticed, so we use Focusing to draw attention to the model and to the particular aspects of his or her performance that are to be imitated.

Mediating. We use Mediating to resolve a conflict when members' positions become somewhat fixed, and the group cannot progress unless the conflict is resolved. The very act of Mediating a conflict draws attention to the fact that a conflict exists which the group needs to resolve.

Starting. When members do not know one another, they need help to get the interactive "juices" flowing. By Focusing on this newness, the group makes it possible to get past introductions, and down to the business of defining its goals and roles so that it can begin to work and become an effective group. Starting also occurs, but in a different sense, when the group's membership changes. In effect, this creates a "new" group, and attention needs to be focused on the ways in which this affects the group's development.

IN PREPARATION

In the exercise for Summarizing, the discussion topic used for the exercise should be a problem you experience in your work or your studies. You can ask one member to present a problem, or ask the group to discuss a common problem that members have experienced, so that the group can discuss alternative ways of resolving that problem. The problem you select should be a real one that is perplexing and likely to be of interest to the group. For example, you might talk about a client or a fellow committee member who is proving particularly difficult; better yet, if you are working with or participating in a group, you might talk about something in the group that is troublesome, such as what to do about someone who is the group's scapegoat, how to handle conflicting subgroups that are competing for control of the group, and so on.

In the Summarizing chapter, the exercise calls for only one presentation, but it is probably a good idea to have more than one person prepared to discuss his or her problem with the class if you decide to work on individual problems. How you select a presenter is up to you: It is probably best to start with volunteers.

You will also need a spinner with numbers, a pair of dice, names written on a slip of paper and dropped in a container of some sort, or any other device by which a member's name can be selected by chance.

NOTES

1. An exception to this attempt to involve members in the management of their own group would be a task group, in which the group's contract calls for the chair to allow no significant straying from the group's agenda.

2. The answer to this problem is given on page 190 of the book. Only the convener should read the answer before the session. Once the observers have been designated during the session, they too can read the answer. Anyone else who peeks will destroy the usefulness of this exercise.

SUGGESTED READINGS

Brown, R. (1986). *Social psychology* (2nd ed.). New York: Free Press.
Goodwin, K., & Turner, R. (1981). Effects of focusing on hypothesis testing in concrete operational children. *International Journal of Behavioral Development, 4*(3), 313-332.
Hahn, S., Croen, L., Kupfer, R., & Levin, G. (1991). A method for teaching human values in clinical clerkships through group discussion. *Teaching and Learning in Medicine, 3*(3), 143-150.
Kernodie, M., & Carlton, L. (1992). Information feedback and the learning of multiple-degree-of-information activities. *Journal of Motor Behavior, 24*(2), 187-196.
Liberman, R., Massel, H., Mosk, M., & Wong, S. (1985). Social skills training for chronic mental patients. *Hospital and Community Psychiatry, 36*(4), 396-403.
Stasser, G., & Stewart, D. (1992). Discovery of hidden profiles by decision-making groups: Solving a problem versus making a judgment. *Journal of Personality and Social Psychology, 63*(3), 426-434.
Winter, M., & Holloway, E. (1991). Relation of trainee experience, conceptual level, and supervisor approach to selection of audiotaped counseling passages. *Clinical Supervisor, 9*(2), 87-103.

Chapter 8

SUMMARIZING

HOW DO YOU DESCRIBE SUMMARIZING?

Summarizing is the process of drawing together and briefly restating a number of prior responses into one statement, then seeking agreement or correction from the group members until a summary statement has been produced that everyone considers accurate.

Describe an example of Summarizing that you have seen recently.

_____

_____

_____

WHEN DO YOU USE SUMMARIZING?

1. You want everyone to start a meeting from the same point, so you summarize previous activities of the group that relate to this session; for example, "I think this is what we decided at our last meeting" or "These are the questions left unanswered from our last meeting." (In a group that keeps minutes, such as a committee, reviewing minutes at the beginning of a meeting is a form of Summarizing.) A variation of this process is to ask one or more members to provide such a summary.

2. Members express confusion about an issue being discussed and ask for a clear statement of the problem, so someone attempts to summarize what the problem is and where the group is in relation to the problem.

3. A topic has been discussed at length and points that have already been made begin to recur, so a summary is made: This allows the group to conclude this step in the discussion and move on to the next step.

4. It is recognized that a subgoal of the group has been reached and closure is needed (via a summary) so that the group can continue.

5. Someone introduces a new topic before the previous one has been settled: Summarizing is then used to determine whether a shift of topic is acceptable to the group.

6. One member has been dominating the discussion and you want to tactfully involve others. Summarizing can be used as one way to interrupt a speaker tactfully so others can have their say (see Gatekeeping).

7. The meeting is concluding and it is appropriate to draw together what has been said or done in order to (a) compare it with the goals of this meeting and (b) lay the basis for the next meeting.

In regard to the example of Summarizing that you described, was it used at the right time? Why do you think so?

_____

_____

_____

HOW DO YOU SUMMARIZE?

With the exception of the *introductory* summary (see above), a good summary *follows* a fair amount of group interaction. If every contribution of each member is summarized, you are Attending, not Summarizing. A good summary is brief, highlights major points of the preceding discussion, and omits references to irrelevancies and small points. It rewards members by identifying them with their contribution (e.g., "As Jane said..."), does not add *new* data to the discussion, and includes a statement that seeks agreement (or correction leading to agreement) from the group (e.g., "Is that a fair review of what we said?").

It is usually preferable to have group members rather than the group Leader summarize: If members know ahead of time that they may be asked to summarize they are more likely to use good Attending behavior. In addition, when members summarize, the Leader gets a feeling for the ways in which group members see what has been happening in the group.

In the example of Summarizing that you have described, was its use effective? Why?

_____

_____

_____

HOW DO YOU KNOW YOU
HAVE USED SUMMARIZING CORRECTLY?

Some indications that you have been summarizing correctly include: the group will agree with the summary statement (verbally, nodding in agreement, and so forth) or will offer corrections and then agree to the revised summary statement; the group moves on to a new topic; old points are not rehashed; everyone's contributions clearly show that they know what has been discussed.

OPPRESSION AND EMPOWERMENT
IN RELATION TO SUMMARIZING

It is often the case that groups are led by professionally trained group workers who are not members of the same population as the members are (e.g., white worker, black members; male worker, female clients; etc.). In other groups, different members within one group may come from a variety of populations, some of whom—but not all—have known a long history of discrimination. In all of these situations, there is a very real possibility that clear communication is complicated by major and subtle differences in the ways people communicate and in the different ways that they perceive what has been communicated. Among some people, for example, eye contact during communication is considered rude and intrusive, while among others, being unwilling to look a person in the eye is associated with someone who is not to be trusted.

In all of these instances, summarizing what has been communicated among members is a good way of checking the degree to which everyone has understood one another. As such, it is critical that the person who summarizes states his or her summary in clear yet tentative terms; for example, "This is what I think I have heard us all say in the last 5 to 10 minutes. Please correct me if I've missed something." Assuming that corrections do occur, this would be a good opportunity to engage the group in a discussion of just what led to the confusion in communication so as to improve the clarity of communication for the future. In addition, it may help to establish the norm that differences among members or between members and the worker may require future efforts to make sure that one is being understood. This kind of caring for one another can only help the group in its development.

AN EXAMPLE OF SUMMARIZING

SCENE

The Child Guidance Clinic provides treatment services to children who are experiencing emotional difficulties and their families. This is the first meeting of a mother's group: All of the mothers have preschool children in a treatment group. The social worker responsible for the group had met with each of the mothers before this meeting took place. None of the women is employed outside of the home. They are in their middle 30s and are middle class. Mrs. Edwards, Mrs. Brown, and Mrs. Smith are white. The worker and Mrs. Lewis are black. Mrs. Smith canceled her attendance at the meeting because her daughter was ill.

ACTION	DISCUSSION
WORKER: Well, why don't we all make ourselves comfortable? I expect Mrs. Lewis will be joining us in a few minutes.	Worker starts the meeting by getting everyone comfortably settled.
MRS. BROWN: Is it all right if I sit here, next to you?	
WORKER: Certainly, Mrs. Brown. Oh, and here's Mrs. Lewis. Hi, Mrs. Lewis, won't you join us? Have you met Mrs. Edwards? Mrs. Brown?	
MRS. LEWIS: No, but I'm pleased to make your acquaintance. I hope I'm not late?	
WORKER: Oh, no, we've just arrived ourselves. Well, ladies, as you all know, each one of you has a child participating in one	Worker uses Summarizing to start the meeting. She is not telling them anything new— just saying it to all of them as a

of our groups. And, as I explained to each of you individually, it's been our experience that parents of children in our program often have good, common-sense advice to give each other, based on experience, as well as support and understanding of the difficulties you're having with your child. In other words, parents can help each other and be helped by participating in a group like this. We usually keep our groups small so that everyone has a chance to be heard. Our fourth member, Mrs. Smith, is ill today, but I expect she'll be joining us next time. So, I suggest we get started today by having each of you tell us about your youngster; for example, why you decided to bring your child to our agency and what you hope will happen as a result of your participating in this group. Mrs. Lewis, the other ladies have already met in the waiting room a few times, but they don't know you. So, I wonder if you'd be willing to start?

MRS. LEWIS: Goodness. Well, sure. OK. Let's see. Well, Danny, he's 7. He's really a darling little boy. He and I used to be very close. He was very affectionate—you know, wanting to climb in my lap all the time, giving me lots of hugs and kisses, that sort of thing. But then his sister was born, and—well—he just hasn't been the same since.

group because she has said this to each of them during a private pregroup conference. Summarizing is used here to present the first portion of the agency's proposed contract for this group.

Mrs. Lewis is a good selection to present a parent's concerns. She is fairly open in her presentation, setting a good example for the others. (See Chapter 11.)

I've tried to be affectionate in all the old ways, but he just pushes me away. I've tried— well—everything: cooking his favorite foods, matching every gift his sister gets with something for him, spending lots of time with him. But no matter what I do, if I give the baby any loving, he gets in a snit. And lately, his temper blow-ups have been terrible! The only things worse are his everlasting sulks. His father and I were just at our wit's end! When we heard about this place, we decided to give it a try. He seems to have begun to like the group here, but at home he's just as hard to live with. It's been terribly upsetting to all of us.

MRS. EDWARDS: Well, we're not having that sort of difficulty with Joannie. She's 6 and an only child. Recently, we've been thinking maybe we should keep it that way. But I wonder if this kind of jealousy isn't perfectly normal. After all, Danny did have you all to himself for almost 6 years, right? And I've seen the same kind of jealousy among my neighbor's kids. Of course, it makes me wonder about having a second. I really don't think I could handle behavior like that.

Mrs. Edwards indicates that her concerns are different. In addition, she gives information: Jealousy among young children is, in her experience, quite normal.

WORKER: I guess it worries you to think about problems of jealousy that could develop if you had a second child. But before we get into some of these questions, why don't we get a little more

The Worker shows she is Attending by Responding to the feelings of Mrs. Edwards, but then moves on to Mrs. Brown, so as to maintain the group's focus on sharing information about themselves.

information about each other?
Mrs. Brown, can you tell us
something about Raymond?

MRS. BROWN: Well, for some
time now, we have been having
trouble with Raymond. He's so
full of energy—seems he's going
to burst. He doesn't have very
good control of his temper, and
when he can't have his way he
kicks, bites, even pushes grown-
ups as well as the other kids. I
mean, when he gets going he can
be a holy terror! I suppose
there's a reason for it but I can't
see it. Why, just the other day he
bit a neighbor's girl and left
teeth marks in her leg—even
broke the skin—all over some
toy in the sandbox.

Mrs. Brown is almost saying,
"Well my kid is worse than both
of yours put together."

MRS. LEWIS: Oh, my!

MRS. BROWN: Oh, that's nothing! Why, just last week when
some of the kids wouldn't let
him into their game, he snatched
their ball away and threw it
down the sewer, then began
throwing rocks at them. I've
never seen a child so determined
to have everything his own way!

WORKER: Well, it's true that
children sometimes express their
feelings very directly and that
they have to learn more acceptable ways of communicating
with others. Often there are reasons behind such behavior and if
we can get a better understanding of these reasons, we can
begin to get a handle on helping

The worker uses Information
Giving (". . . children sometimes
express feelings . . .") to suggest another part of the contract. Then she asks the members
to give information about their
observations of other children.

the child. I wonder, for example, if any of you have ever seen a child act like Mrs. Brown's description of Raymond?

MRS. LEWIS: Well, my next-door neighbor's second oldest used to kick his mother when he was angry at her, but he did it because his mother was always right and he was wrong.

Mrs. Lewis's response to the worker's question gives some support to Mrs. Brown.

MRS. BROWN: Yes, well, there is something else about Raymond. I have a terrible problem getting him to eat the kinds of food he should.

Mrs. Brown doesn't respond to Mrs. Lewis's comment. Instead, she introduces a new topic: her difficulty with Raymond concerning food.

MRS. LEWIS: Me, too. No matter what I give Danny, he finds fault.

Another mother gives information about her problems with food. This is probably reassuring to Mrs. Brown; she is not the only one with this problem.

MRS. EDWARDS: Dinner time has always been painful for us, too. Joanne seems to think food is a toy to be played with, not eaten. She dawdles so, and lately she's become so terribly finicky about what she will and won't eat.

MRS. BROWN: Well, you know, that's very interesting because Raymond—well, he'll go for candy, sugar-coated cereal, things like that, but eggs or chicken or even steak—he won't eat those things, no matter how I prepare them.

WORKER: Well, OK, I wonder if I could try pulling together what we've said so far, to see if

The Worker sums up the issues each of the members has presented as a way of setting the

I'm hearing you correctly. Obviously, each of you has some specific concerns about your child—like Danny's jealousy toward his sister—that is unique for you. But it's also clear that you all share some problems in common—like the way your kids handle eating. It's quite possible that you've blamed yourself that these problems exist, or have been blamed by others for causing these problems to develop. In either case, you clearly feel uncomfortable about the way things are going with your youngsters and would like it to change.

group's future agenda. In doing so, she tries to individualize her comments while at the same time drawing attention to the underlying similarities of the members' concerns.

MRS. BROWN: You better believe it!

MRS. LEWIS: Yes.

MRS. EDWARDS: Um-hmm.

WORKER: OK. Are there some other things that are proving difficult?

As the meeting continued, the women shared concerns about the use of punishment, about their own feelings of anger at their children. In this process, they created an agenda for future meetings. The meeting ended with expressions of satisfaction about having the opportunity to express their concerns in an atmosphere of group acceptance.

EXERCISE

Goal

When participating in a group meeting, you should be able to summarize what the members have said or done in a way that these members would say, if asked, is both fair and complete. Further, you should be able to use Summarizing often enough to facilitate group movement, without using unnecessary summaries in a way that interferes with group interaction.

Time Required

   Varies with the problem to be solved.

Materials

   A spinner with numbers, a pair of dice, names written on slips of paper and dropped in a container of some sort, or any other device by which a member's name can be selected by chance.

Specialized Roles

   At the beginning of the exercise, one of the members is to use one of the devices suggested above to select the name of a member by chance. He or she will call out the name of the person selected. He or she is not to operate the device again until either (a) the Summarizer summarizes and the group accepts the summary or corrects it until it is acceptable or (b) 5 minutes go by without a summary by the Summarizer. The Summarizer should not feel compelled to summarize if nothing happens worth summarizing. At points (a) or (b) the member using the selection device will do so again to designate a new Summarizer. (The same Summarizer might be selected by chance to repeat his or her role, but only once.) Each new Summarizer attempts to introduce a summary at an appropriate point and has 5 minutes from the time his or her name is called to do so.

Process

   As indicated at the end of the write-up on Focusing, the group should try to solve a work problem of one or more of its members. Because the role of Summarizer may fall on anyone, each member should be attentive. After everyone has had a turn as Summarizer, or the problem has been resolved to the presenter's satisfaction, stop the discussion and review the experience.

POSTSCRIPT:
ISSUES IN SUMMARIZING

   The trick in Summarizing is to know *when* Summarizing should be used: too early and it may cut off discussion that's necessary to reach group consensus, but too late may allow a group to "spin its wheels" unnecessarily, causing some members to lose interest, while for the group-as-a-whole, precious time may be wasted. How can you tell when Summarizing should occur?

First, it is almost always a good idea to start all but the first meeting with a summary of what happened at the last meeting. This provides a foundation for this meeting by establishing what was done and defining what remains to be done.

Second, if the group has set out to solve a particular group problem, or deal with one member's issue, and the group's Leader believes that either has been satisfactorily resolved, it helps to check this out by asking members to summarize what they believe has been accomplished. In this way, you can assess member perceptions of the group's activity to date, and perhaps prepare the group for moving on to its next item of business.

Third, if the issue being dealt with is complicated, it can be helpful to work for consensus on what has been achieved so far (by the use of Summarizing) even when the group is still in the midst of problem solving. Summarizing at *this* point is an attempt to ask the group if there is agreement on some beginning steps in the problem-solving process (assuming that the person using Summarizing believes that this kind of consensus has been achieved). It is also possible that the group has stalled because of a basic disagreement. In this case, Mediating may need to be used to resolve the disagreement. If so, the first step in the process of Mediating is the use of Summarizing, to make sure that everyone agrees on the nature of the disagreement.

Finally, Summarizing should be used to conclude a meeting, rather than simply letting things drift off to some vague conclusion. In this way, members are clear on what has been accomplished and on what remains to be done. This can help members conclude their meeting by planning for the next meeting.

Who does the Summarizing is another important issue. In some cases, a group might agree that members will take turns, at the beginning or end of the meeting at least, to use Summarizing. Members who know they will be responsible for a complete and accurate summary of a particular meeting could be expected to attend carefully to group process. Further, where the group has a formal leader, the summaries of members provides that leader with a way of sampling members' perceptions of the group. A leader who spots an incomplete or inaccurate summary should look first to the other members for corrections or additions, because this is another way of assessing member perceptions of the group's processes. Ultimately, however, if members' summaries are inaccurate or incomplete (in the Leader's opinion) and no one else appears to recognize this, the Leader will need to provide a corrected summary, and then check with the group to make sure that he or she has not misperceived group activity.

IN PREPARATION

To prepare for the exercise in the chapter on Gatekeeping, you will need the tape recording of your Contract Negotiation session, and a tape recorder to play it. In addition, a chalkboard (with chalk and eraser) or a newsprint pad with thick black felt pen and a watch with a sweep second hand will be needed. Finally, you will need to select a portion of the tape for analysis because there may not be enough time to replay the tape of the entire exercise, then review the data made in coding that behavior. In selecting that portion of the tape, choose 15 to 20 minutes during which several members participated.

SUGGESTED READINGS

Christensen, E. (1983). Study circles: Learning in small groups. *Journal for Specialists in Group Work, 8*(4), 211-217.

Gajira, M., & Salvia, J. (1992). The effects of summarization training on text comprehension of students with learning disabilities. *Exceptional Children, 58*(6), 508-516.

Johnson, D. (1991). *Joining together: Group theory and group skills* (4th ed.). Boston: Allyn & Bacon.

King, A. (1992). Comparison of self-questioning, summarizing, and note-taking review as strategies for learning from lectures. *American Educational Research Journal, 29*(2), 303-323.

McAdam, E. (1986). Cognitive behaviour therapy and its application with adolescents. *Journal of Adolescence, 9*(1), 1-15.

McKeachie, W. (1986). *Teaching tips: A guidebook for the beginning college teacher* (8th ed.). Lexington, MA: Heath.

Yager, S., Johnson, D., & Johnson, R. (1985). Oral discussion, group-to-individual transfer, and achievement in cooperative learning groups. *Journal of Educational Psychology, 77*(1), 60-66.

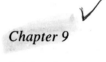

Chapter 9

GATEKEEPING

HOW DO YOU DESCRIBE GATEKEEPING?

Gatekeeping is behavior that helps all members of the group participate more or less equally by limiting those members who monopolize the discussion and by encouraging low participators to talk more. Although no group achieves total equality of participation among its members, Gatekeeping is used to achieve a fairly equitable distribution of participation among all members.

What is an example of Gatekeeping you have seen recently?

_____

_____

_____

WHEN DO YOU GATEKEEP?

After about one fourth of the meeting time, if you observe that:

1. one or two members have dominated the conversation,

AUTHOR'S NOTE: In some fields (i.e., community mental health) the term *gatekeeping* has been used in reference to the process used by people who facilitate *linkages* between organizations or between individuals in need of some resources and organizations that can provide these resources. The use of the term *gatekeeping* in this guide is clearly in a different vein, because it speaks to both "opening" and "closing" the gate where the term *gate* refers to access to participation within the group.

2. some members have not participated at all, and/or

3. most comments are directed at the Leader of the group with little interaction among members, so that he or she is speaking a great deal more than any of the other participants,

then it is time to use Gatekeeping. In a group where membership changes slowly or not at all, you will find that certain people tend to participate in a predictable way. At that point, you may not want to wait until one fourth of the meeting has gone by to gatekeep. In other words, it may be necessary to intervene earlier before certain less-productive patterns of participation become too fixed.

In the example of Gatekeeping that you have described, was it used at the appropriate time? Why do you think so?

HOW DO YOU GATEKEEP?

Early in the life of the group, when negotiating the group's contract, discuss the importance of participation as a way of fostering the group's development. Members should be encouraged to gatekeep for themselves and for others, rather than relying on the Leader to do it all the time. Everyone should scan the group from time to time to keep track of those who vary widely from a fairly equal share of "talk time." When scanning, watch for nonverbal "I-want-to-participate" cues from "undertalkers" (e.g., leaning forward, an abrupt change in facial expression, starting to speak but getting cut off, etc.).

Always combine limitations of overtalkers with invitations to undertalkers. For example, "That's a good point, John. What do some of the rest of you think about that?" (Pause—then, if there are no takers, "Pete, how about you?".) Be sure to praise contributions of undertalkers, particularly when you think their low level of participation is a result of shyness, uncertainty, or low status in the group.[1]

Some notes of caution:

1. Be careful not to give undue praise if the contribution is off-topic because that will reward off-topic remarks. If it is made by a low participator, however, reward the fact of participation and then try to relate the remark to the topic.

2. Be careful to gatekeep impartially so that members do not think you are encouraging people you like or whose positions agree with yours, while ignoring or suppressing those you are not as close to or whose positions disagree with yours.

3. Some people say little but what they say is to the point and a valuable contribution to the group. Accordingly, it is important to make allowances for the low-participation style of some members.

4. The participation style of some members may be self-defeating in nature, and it may be appropriate to negotiate a private or group contract with some individuals to help them work on changing their style of participation. In that case, Gatekeeping serves as a reminder of the contract. For example, John knows that he is long-winded and tends to speak at great length, "unless somebody shuts me up." In this case John wants to learn how to express himself more succinctly because his lengthy comments tend to bore his listeners. Gatekeeping signals him that he is talking too much again, something he wants to change. The signal could be agreed on ahead of time as a look, a wink, a hand signal, and so on.

In the example of Gatekeeping that you have described, was it used effectively? Why do you think so?

_____

_____

_____

HOW DO YOU KNOW YOU HAVE USED
GATEKEEPING SUCCESSFULLY?

1. All members contribute to the discussion to a fairly equal degree, as measured by the frequency and length of statements;
2. Members report (if asked) that they are satisfied with the participation levels within the group, including their own;
3. Members address comments and questions to one another during a meeting instead of focusing the majority of their comments on one person. In addition, members encourage silent members to speak and they ignore monopolizers or assist in controlling them;
4. Members who contract to change their participation styles make progress toward their participation goals as a result of Gatekeeping.

OPPRESSION AND EMPOWERMENT
IN RELATION TO GATEKEEPING

In mixed groups (e.g., men and women, Caucasians and African-Americans, etc.), there are often individuals who identify with one population that has traditionally been forced to occupy a lower status in society than another population. Thus, for example, the old saying, "A woman's place is in the home," was also meant to suggest "in the home and quietly in the background."

Placed in a group that emphasizes equality in all matters (e.g., right and responsibility to participate, right and responsibility to dissent as one feels the need to do so, etc.), the group worker often has to give considerable attention to achieving a generally equal level of participation among all members of this mixed group. Individuals who have been taught to "know their place" and say nothing to attract attention to themselves can suddenly be faced with a group worker who expects them to participate. And someone who expects to be able to be dominant in many social situations (and who has come to assume this) may encounter a group worker who will not allow that to happen in *this* group.

The group worker who uses Gatekeeping to achieve a balance of participation in a mixed group has to recognize that both the traditionally low and traditionally high participating members are likely to experience this "equal participation" norm with some difficulty. In fact, the group worker may have a struggle when attempting to build this form of equality into the group's contract. In doing so, the group worker may want to explain why it may be difficult for everyone to achieve this kind of balanced participation and how, in the long run, the worker believes this can be of benefit to both the group-as-a-whole and to each individual member. Then the Worker needs to gently, but firmly, help the group operate according to this norm. This could include reminding the group about why it is important to hear from the less active members, and equally, why it is important for the talkative members to improve their listening skills.

AN EXAMPLE OF GATEKEEPING

SCENE

Herbert Marshall, a psychiatrist in private practice, is conducting the second meeting of a therapy group. The group consists of five adults—

two men and three women—who are experiencing emotional difficulties in their lives.

> Midge: 29, single, small and easily frightened, a secretary in an insurance firm
>
> Larry: 40, divorced, aloof, tense, a librarian at a local small college
>
> Martin: 23, single, disorganized, emotional, a graduate student at the University, majoring in Business Administration
>
> Ann: 35, married but separated, tense, critical, a computer technician
>
> Rachel: 32, single, shy, unexpressive, an elementary school teacher

When the meeting began, Dr. Marshall asked the group if anyone wanted to share their reactions to the first meeting. After several false starts, Midge described her profound feelings of emptiness after the last meeting.

ACTION	DISCUSSION
MIDGE: After I left the meeting I just walked and walked and I just felt hollow. Empty. As if there was no "me" left. I got home, somehow. But being there didn't help. And then [her voice becomes tearful] I began to cry. I don't know why. I just cried and cried and cried [tears start falling as she speaks].	Midge lays her feelings bare before the group and her feelings begin to overwhelm her again.
MARTIN: That must have felt awful.	Several members respond sympathetically to Midge's distress.
RACHEL: You must have felt all alone.	
MIDGE: [Wiping away the tears and trying to smile, but the tears continue to fall.] It was so silly, all that crying.	Midge is trying to be brave but is still in the grip of a powerful emotion—even more so because of the expression of concern from others.
LARRY: [The longer Larry speaks the more the group fidgets, restlessly.] Well, I had a very different reaction, if you	Finally, Ann spots her chance to break in when Larry poses a rhetorical question and pauses for a breath.

want to know. The group wasn't
anything like what I had expected. I mean I thought we'd
get more information about the
dynamics of human behavior—
the kind of information you
could use for insight development. And it made me wonder
about group psychotherapy. Is it
really effective? I mean, has it
been carefully researched? Because I couldn't see how a group
can take the place of an intense
and meaningful relationship between an individual and a therapist. And I asked myself, doesn't
the group get in the way of the
therapist's getting to know you—
I mean, really know where
you're coming from? Each one
of us, after all, is so different
from the other.

ANN: Different, yes, Larry, but
maybe that's a plus factor. Because there may be some experience that—oh, say—Martin has
had that can help me and vice
versa.

This is a member's first attempt
at Gatekeeping. She attempts to
answer his question. But because he really doesn't want an
answer, it doesn't work. What
he wants is some way to ignore
Midge's tears.

LARRY: I don't see how. It
seems to me . . .

Larry wants to continue his intel-
lectual review of group therapy.

MARTIN: I do. Like some of
you have been married. I never
have. I think I could learn a lot
from hearing you all talk about
it. But Midge, I do agree with
you that—well—sometimes you
wonder what you're doing here,
and what difference would it
make to anyone if you weren't
here . . .

Martin, emboldened by Ann, in-
terrupts, gives his opinion, and
then uses Focusing to return the
group's attention to Midge.

RACHEL: I once cried like that—on and on. It was on my ninth birthday. Nothing went right. I've never forgotten that.

Rachel elaborates on her understanding of the way Midge feels.

ANN: Well—but crying isn't always a bad thing, is it, Dr. Marshall?

Ann recognizes the value in tears. She also plays the role of "good girl" by turning to the "all-knowing" Dr. Marshall who had remained silent to that point. Perhaps she is uncomfortable with his silence and is, in effect, Gatekeeping (to involve this particular low participant, Dr. Marshall) via Information Seeking, to get him to become more active (and dominant) in the group.

DR. MARSHALL: That's right, Ann. It's a way of getting your feelings out. And when feelings are expressed, we can work on them. I am interested, though, Larry, that you seem to have been less affected by Midge's crying than the others.

Now that the group has shown its ability to use Gatekeeping, Dr. Marshall steps in to support Ann's point. But he senses that Larry's lengthy comment may have been his attempt to defend against his own feelings of turmoil when faced with the intensity of Midge's feelings. So, Dr. Marshall decides to test Larry's awareness of his own defenses. Perhaps this is an area that Larry will want to work on. Note that Dr. Marshall presents this as an observation rather than as an accusation.

LARRY: Yes. Well—yes. Well, I guess you're right. Bull's-eye! Score one for you, Dr. Marshall. I just don't let other people's emotions get to me. People have told me that. And sometimes— well, it's gotten me in trouble in the past.

Larry recognizes that his reaction was different from that of the others. His reply is sarcastic—like a boy caught with his hand in the cookie jar, but he's smart enough to know, intellectually, that this is precisely what he is paying Dr. Marshall to do. And in fact, as he thinks about it, he is troubled by this awareness.

DR. MARSHALL: Perhaps that's something you'd like to work on in the group.

Dr. Marshall proposes an individual contract to Larry in front of the group so that it can become part of the group's contract.

LARRY: Hmmm. Yes. Yes. [Thoughtful] That might be something to work on. In the group. Hmm.

Larry agrees, at least for the moment, but his tentative reply suggests that he may simply be trying to get out of the limelight.

The group then refocused on the events in the first meeting that were associated with Midge's feeling of emptiness. Later they moved on to consider Larry's distancing of himself from Midge's expression of troubled feelings.

EXERCISE

Goals

When participating in a group, you will be able to recognize when members' participation (including your own) are unequal to a significant degree, and based on that recognition to (a) invite the participation of low participators, (b) help to control the over-participation of some, and where needed, (c) modify your own behavior accordingly, until there is a regular pattern of shared participation involving all members.

In particular, this exercise will help you learn to:

1. Practice the coding of group interaction to become more aware of the ways in which individuals participate in a group.
2. Increase your ability to recognize a variety of situations in which Gatekeeping is needed and to become familiar with a number of Gatekeeping methods.
3. Review the Contract the group negotiated to determine its relevance for the current operations of your group.

Materials

1. Pencils and a watch or clock with a sweep second hand
2. An audio- or videotape recorder and the tape recording of the exercise from the group's Contract Negotiation session
3. A chalkboard or newsprint pad on which to record a summary of observations for all to see

Time Required

About half of the time remaining (after discussing this chapter) for playback and analysis of some portion of the tape that has been preselected for review.

Specialized Roles

As you listen to the tape recording, you are to code the verbal participation of **one** person (other than yourself) who was present during the Contract Negotiation session.

Process

As you recall, you recorded your discussion when you negotiated your own contract as a group. The group should now listen to a preselected portion of that tape so that each member has the experience of measuring and analyzing the participation of one member and the amount and nature of Gatekeeping performed by that person during the discussion.

Try to determine whether the person you are listening to spoke to the group as a whole, to another individual, or to the formal leader, and approximately how long he or she spoke each time he or she spoke. Decide whether the comment included an attempt to use Gatekeeping. A sample coding of Dr. Marshall's group has been included to show you how this is done (see Table 9.1).

Analysis

Although the sample is very short, some issues relevant to Gatekeeping emerge. Dr. Marshall, the Leader, is a low participant and is spoken to by only two members. Gatekeeping is used by Ann and Martin to cut into Larry's participation. So far, no one has spoken to Martin or Rachel. More comments are addressed to the group as a whole than to individuals, and so forth. This sample analytical device suggests several interesting comparisons. For example, does the person who speaks the most have the most comments directed to him or her? Is there any evidence that the person who speaks the most has more (or less) influence in the group than any other participant?

As you listen to the tape, stop it when necessary to determine who spoke, if it is unclear. At times this may be difficult—particularly with audiotape—but do the best you can. Total your observations, then report them to the group so that everyone sees the data for the entire group.

Now discuss your observations. It might be helpful for members to try to recall their opinions and feelings about the amounts of participation by

TABLE 9.1 Who-to-Whom Chart, Based on the Example for Gatekeeping

| Speaker | Total Group | Spoken to | | | | | | Total Comments | Total Gatekeeping Attempts |
		Midge	Martin	Ann	Rachel	Larry	Dr. Marshall		
Midge	9	X	0	0	0	0*	0	9	0
Martin	3	2 (1*)	X	0	0	1*	0	6	2
Ann	0	0	0	X	0	2 (1*)	1*	3	2
Rachel	4	1	0	0	X	0	0	5	0
Larry	9	0	0	1	0	X	14	24	0
Dr. Marshall	0	0	0	3	0	2 (2*)	X	5	2
TOTALS	25	3	0	4	0	5	15	52	6

NOTE: In coding a live group (or one on audio- or videotape), assign one tic mark (') for every 15 seconds that the person is speaking without interruption and one tic mark for a fraction of 15 seconds. Thus if the participant speaks for about 40 seconds, you would assign three tic marks to that statement. (In this sample, because I am working from typed script, I have assigned one tic mark to every sentence.) Eventually, add all tic marks together for a participant's total.

* The comment(s) was (were) a Gatekeeping attempt.

123

themselves and others in the Contract Negotiation session. In addition, you could compare your measurements of participation during the Contract Negotiation session with your assessment of the kind of contract you negotiated. For example, were the people who participated most in that session the same ones who were most satisfied with the outcomes of that session? Or, what relationship, if any, have you found to exist between levels of participation in the Contract Negotiation session and opinions about the contract as it is operating today? Have you noted a significant shift in levels of participation by individual participants in the group since the Contract Negotiation session? If so, how has this affected the group's development as a group? If levels of participation have *not* changed significantly, what has this stability meant to the group? And so forth.

Also, pay particular attention to attempts to use Gatekeeping during the segment of tape you coded. The Gatekeeping attempts may have taken several forms, such as Information Seeking or Summarizing. Also, see if there were any occasions in which a participant was inadvertently gatekeeping; that is, a participant's contribution did not appear to be designed to encourage or discourage other speakers, but had the effect of doing so.

Discuss the implications of your observations for the use of Gatekeeping. You may want to note the ways in which Gatekeeping differs from, but is relevant to, Focusing or to some of the other techniques that have been presented and, as in all of your discussions, how this applies to work with groups in which you play a leadership or membership role.

POSTSCRIPT:
ISSUES IN GATEKEEPING

The observation and analysis of small group interaction has occupied the attention of many scholars. Among them, the work of Robert Bales (1955) is particularly noteworthy. He developed a method by which observers could code the behaviors of group participants into one of twelve discrete categories called Interaction Process Analysis (IPA). Half of these categories focused on task activities of group members (i.e., working to achieve group goals) and half dealt with socioemotional aspects of group interaction (i.e., members' feelings about their interactions). Over time, Bales' method came to be used widely for small group analysis.

More recently, Bales created a more complex scheme, Systematic Multiple Level Observation of Groups (SYMLOG), for the analysis of small group interaction (Bales, 1980; Bales, Cohen, & Williamson, 1979). IPA focuses on the difference between task and socioemotional behaviors. SYMLOG describes these two factors as two ends of a continuum of "role structure behaviors" that, together, comprise one of *three* dimensions by which group interactions could be described and analyzed; the other two are "status" (dominance/submission) and "attraction" (friendly/unfriendly).

Both IPA and SYMLOG require significant amounts of training for observers. In addition, they involve fairly time-consuming processes. Recently, these issues have been addressed by the application of computer technology to the coding and analysis processes (Losada & Markovitch, 1990). At this writing, the use of this innovation is quite limited, with a focus on improving the effectiveness of group interaction among business executives. The developmental work is being conducted in Ann Arbor, and I plan to remain in close touch with this exciting approach.

IN PREPARATION

Square the number of members in your group. Then multiply that result by 2. That is the number of blank 3-by-5 cards you will need for the Confrontation exercise. Also, have enough ballpoint pens of the *same color* for every member of the group.

NOTE

1. See the post script at the end of this chapter for an examination of the many factors that can explain undertalking.

SUGGESTED READINGS

Bertcher, H. (1987). Effective group membership. *Social Work With Groups, 10*(2), 57-67.
Counselman, E. (1991). Leadership in a long-term leaderless woman's group. *Small Group Research, 22*(2), 240-257.
Fielding, J. (1983). Verbal participation and group therapy outcome. *British Journal of Psychiatry, 142,* 524-528.
Shen, W., Sanchez, A., & Huang, T. (1984). Verbal participation in group therapy: A comparative study on New Mexico ethnic groups. *Hispanic Journal of Behavioral Sciences, 6*(3), 277-284.
Vinokur, A., Burnstein, E., Sechrest, L., & Wortman, P. (1985). *Journal of Personality and Social Psychology, 49*(1), 70-84.

Chapter 10

CONFRONTATION

HOW DO YOU DESCRIBE CONFRONTATION?

In *Confrontation*, an individual is *informed* of an inconsistency (a) between something he or she has said or done and something else he or she has said or done or (b) between something he or she has said or done and fact. In other words, it is a specialized form of Information Giving that is used to *compel individuals* to change their behavior, because they experience the inconsistency as intolerable in their effort to make sense out of their reality. Confrontation can compel an individual to reconsider and make a change in behavior that others find unacceptable, because the individual is being inconsistent; for example, "You say that you're ready to trust the group with your problem, but every time something goes wrong at home you keep it to yourself and we only hear about it when it's too late for us to help," or "You've repeatedly said you want to see more cooperative interaction between our organizations, but whenever we come up with a specific proposal to make that happen, you oppose it." In the latter example, a representative of one organization is being informed by someone from another organization that his words and actions are inconsistent in that they violate an underlying norm of honesty in the exchanges between their respective organizations. It should be added that Confrontation need not be limited to an individual: Several individuals or the entire group could be the target of Confrontation.

What is an example of Confrontation that you have seen recently?

WHEN DO YOU USE CONFRONTATION?

1. The participant's inconsistent behavior is getting him or her in trouble with the group or with a life situation; for example, a member who has spoken infrequently in the group complains that people always ignore her wishes, without recognizing that she rarely tells people what she wants; or members are annoyed because the chairperson always speaks of starting on time but usually arrives late.

2. The participant does not appear to realize that there is an inconsistency in his or her behavior and therefore does nothing about it; or the group—or part of the group—is behaving in a way that is inconsistent with its contract and has made no effort to change its contract accordingly.

3. An important point about timing: Confrontation is not likely to work unless the member, subgroup, or group that is confronted has agreed to a contract with regard to this group. Accordingly, you should only use Confrontation after the contract has been negotiated.

In regard to your example of Confrontation, was it used at the appropriate time? Why do you think so?

_____

_____

_____

HOW DO YOU USE CONFRONTATION?

It often helps to remind the participant(s) of that portion of the contract that is related to the inconsistency you hope to eliminate and of his or her (or their) earlier agreement to that contract. This helps to make the Confrontation an effort to achieve a goal that they agreed to work toward, rather than a personal attack.

When using Confrontation, relax physically so that you are in a comfortable position. Avoid actions or words that could be perceived by the participant(s) as critical or attacking. Use your normal tone of voice in *informing* (rather than accusing) the participant(s) of the inconsistency you see. Members are often **more** emotional when Confronting one another than a Leader is, and that is okay, but persons in a formal position of leadership should try to present a constructive, friendly approach.

It is best to be brief: Limit your statement to a few sentences. State exactly what the discrepant behavior and/or information is, without explanation or apologies. Experience has shown that it is often necessary to repeat a Confrontation (albeit not using the exact same words) a number of times—gently, but firmly—before some individuals will see or accept the inconsistency in what they are saying or doing. If you think that the inconsistency you have selected is apparent to other participants, you should ask them to present their views on this matter, including examples of the discrepant behavior.

Asking the group to confront one member can lead to people isolating that member and making him or her a scapegoat. Sometimes participants dodge major issues by applying unnecessarily severe pressure to one member, blaming him or her for what they perceive as the group's failure. When and if this happens, it may be necessary for some participants to confront the rest of the group with the discrepancy between the group's contract concerning such things as mutual helpfulness or goal achievement, and their overemphasis on one member's inconsistencies.

Remember that the purpose of Confrontation is an addition to one or more participant's contract with the group. You want them to realize that a discrepancy exists, and you want them to agree to work on reducing the discrepancy. To achieve these ends, you would probably benefit by *avoiding arguments* with the participant you have confronted if he or she disagrees about the discrepancy you have highlighted; instead, stick to your Information Giving approach.

In the example of Confrontation that you have described, was it used effectively? Why?

HOW DO YOU KNOW YOU HAVE USED
CONFRONTATION SUCCESSFULLY?

The words and actions of the participant(s) become more consistent with one another over time, regarding the previous inconsistency, or the words and actions of the participant(s) become more consistent with facts.

OPPRESSION AND EMPOWERMENT
IN RELATION TO CONFRONTATION

I have often found that in groups composed of members who are all from the same oppressed population (e.g., all Jewish) a remark or action that might be considered insulting (when made by a member of another population group) is treated as a joke. But in the realities of group work practice, members are often mixed (with regard to such things as race, religion, gender, ethnicity, etc.). When that happens, a member may unintentionally say or do things that members from another population within the group find offensive. When that happens, the group worker may need to confront the individual who made the offensive remark, or performed the offensive act, and confront them with the inconsistency between what they have said and some objective reality or group norm.

A case in point occurred when the planning committee for a school of social work's December graduation decided to decorate the stage with poinsettia flowers. This initially innocent decision was soon challenged by Jewish nonmembers of the group who were planning to graduate at that December ceremony. They saw the poinsettia as a flower generally linked to the celebration of Christmas, a Christian holiday, and asked that some other flower be used instead so that the graduation ceremony not appear to favor any one religion. This precipitated quite an uproar, in which the members of the graduation committee protested, saying the poinsettia is not in any official way connected to any one religion, while the Jewish students claimed that it was.

This committee had no group worker providing leadership, but I like to think a group worker might have used Confrontation by saying something such as,

> Because poinsettias flood the stores every year during the Christmas season, they *have* become informally linked to Christmas—a Christian holiday—over the years. And as a school, we have tried to champion diversity and equality for all. We encourage everyone to avoid doing anything that could be damaging to someone as it relates to their identification with a particular population group. In this situation, our Jewish students experience the selection of this particular flower as offensive to *them*. It seems inconsistent for the school to champion the idea that no group should be made to feel hurt, put down, or discriminated against (and a group in our midst says this is precisely how they are feeling) on the one hand, with the graduation committee's feeling that it ought to be able to create a ceremony in any way it wishes, regardless of who is offended by its decisions.

It is quite likely that this initial use of Confrontation would not solve the problem, and the disagreement would probably continue. A group worker would need to reiterate the inconsistency that was inherently manifest in this situation, and reiterate it in several different ways. Hopefully, this inconsistency would, eventually, be apparent to all, and the committee would voluntarily alter its plans regarding flowers at the graduation.

AN EXAMPLE OF CONFRONTATION

SCENE

The Cobras are what the city police call a "fighting gang"; that is, one that fights other gangs and engages in a variety of antisocial acts, from property destruction or intimidation of others, to grand theft and murder. Composed largely of Hispanic males, ages 14 to 17, the size of the group varies from time to time, although the core group is 10. Groups, Inc., is a small United Fund-supported agency developed to provide a range of social services to such groups—male and female— through the activities of street gang workers. One such worker is Hank, who has been working with the Cobras for about 6 months. In that time he has developed a good relationship with the members. They have indicated that they are interested in taking on the semblance of a social club and are using Hank (who they refer to as their "sponsor") to help them achieve some respectability. With his help, they have been holding meetings in the main building of a nearby city park. The group has sponsored one successful dance, taken an all-day trip to the beach, and participated briefly in the park's football league. Local police have informed Hank that the group's "malicious mischief" has tapered off recently. Nevertheless, Hank has had frequent contacts with the police, and with several probation officers, concerning individual boys who have gotten in trouble.

From the first, Hank knew that the boys used beer, wine, glue sniffing, lighter fluid sniffing, and marijuana to get high. Because the community's recreational resources are severely limited, Hank is concerned that the use of these substances will become a primary means of having a good time and may in time lead the boys to experiment with addicting drugs, if they have not already done so. Last week, however, marijuana posed a new problem. Denny, the group's elected president, was so high on marijuana that he could not conduct a sensible meeting. And Denny had company—six or seven other boys, including all of the group's elected officers. The major business of the meeting was to develop plans for a 5-day camping trip to a national park in the northern part of the state. Groups, Inc., frequently sponsors such trips during the summer for the groups they work with, and when Hank first suggested it, the boys were very enthusiastic. But in the meeting, Denny and the other officers giggled, laughed, and acted silly, so no planning could be done, and the meeting ended in a shambles.

Prior to the next formal meeting at the park, Hank drove to the housing project where many of the boys live. As he pulled up in his car he saw several of the boys sitting on a low retaining wall smoking and chatting, waiting for his arrival and the start of their meeting. Hank noticed some friendly horse play: Several of the boys had spring-clip clothes pins and would attempt to sneak up behind a victim and attach the clothes pin to him without his knowing it. Whenever the boys were successful, there was great hilarity. The victim usually turned out to be the boy who had just arrived and did not know what was going on.

Boys present at this time were:

Denny: Club President (term of office - 3 months)
Jose: Vice President (formerly President)
Corky: Most respected group member
Juan: Sergeant-at-arms
Eliseo: Treasurer
Rafael: A member
Cutter: A member
Thomas: A member

A few minutes after his arrival, Hank was clothespinned and joined in the laughter. As the laughter subsided he put a question to the group:

ACTION	*DISCUSSION*
HANK: Well, have you guys done any more thinking about the camping trip?	Hank knows that the group really wants to go. So he has decided to push the issue in order to show them the inconsistency between effective group problem solving and getting high whenever they feel like it. He knows that their lifestyle will probably not permit them to give up these substances, but he wants them to begin thinking about the distinction between appropriate and inappropriate times for getting high.

JOSE: [Pretending to be a serious professor type.] Hey there, Mr. Hank, sir! What dates have you picked for this fantastic trip to the edge of nowhere?

HANK: No dates yet, Jose. Depends on you guys—

CORKY: Well, it better be soon! I've already borrowed some fishing tackle for the trip. Pan-fried fish right out of the stream! Mmmm, good! I'll show you *vatos* [guys] how to fish.

Corky, as usual, is putting pressure on Hank to do just what the group wants. Hank knows he cannot do that and retain the respect of the members.

THOMAS: Me, I want to see a bear. You're sure there are bears there?

HANK: You better believe it, but you may not want to see one up close.

DENNY: So when do we go? [An aside to Thomas.] Hey man, gimme a *frajo* [cigarette; Thomas gives him one and Denny lights it from Thomas's lit cigarette.]

HANK: Well, it's up to you guys—to plan it. We gotta figure out a lot of things. Not only when we go, but what food we take, who cooks, who does KP—

Hank begins to confront them with the dilemma: getting high and making plans do not mix. These are inconsistent behaviors. To set the stage for Confrontation, he begins to describe the need for thoughtful planning.

CORKY: I cook. He [pointing to Eliseo] does the KP.

ELISEO: [Scowling.] Drop dead, freak.

HANK: Well, actually there's plenty of work; everyone is gonna' have a turn at just about every job. But we can't go un-

Hank further establishes the need for careful planning, and then introduces the problem the group had last week.

less we figure these things out, as a group. And that'll never happen if we have more meetings like last week.

DENNY: Oh, yeah. Well, look, Mr. Hank. You know, we was just having fun. I mean when Thomas blew his nose—like, well, you know, we all cracked up. Thomas, you got the loudest nose in the country!

Denny begins to see what Hank is driving at, but so far, he sees no problem.

THOMAS: [Bowing] Thank you. Thank you.

HANK: It's a great nose, Thomas. But—uh, was it the nose or was it—the pot? I mean, when I got here, you guys were higher'n kites!

Hank puts the issue squarely before the group.

JOSE: Aw, Mr. Hank, it was just—well, you know, we was feelin' good, that's all.

Jose is about as ashamed as the boy caught stealing cookies that he believed were his cookies anyway.

HANK: Boy, you can say that again. [Jose starts to repeat what he said.] No, Jose! I was only kidding. Look, the simple fact is; you can't smoke pot and, at the same time, run a meeting in which you try to plan a trip.

Hank confronts the group with the inconsistency of saying you want to do something that takes planning and then getting so high you cannot possibly plan it.

CORKY: Hey, man, what's wrong with pot? It makes you feel happy. That's all. Not like beer. Beer has a dead kick.

Corky tries to justify their actions. He does not see any inconsistency in what they have done.

HANK: What I mean is—you can't have it both ways. On the one hand, you guys say you really want to go on this trip. Fine. Me, too. But on the other hand, when we get together to work it out, you've been so busy blasting

Hank restates his main point in order to emphasize it. He reminds them of their own intentions and desires—to go, as a group, on the trip. He contrasts this with their behavior when planning needed to be done.

[smoking marijuana] that nothing happens except that everybody cracks up.

THOMAS: But, Mr. Hank, we
was just laughin'. No harm in
that?

Thomas may be beginning to
understand what Hank is trying
to get them to see.

HANK: Thomas, I've been on
a lot of camping trips. Unless
everybody pitches in and does
their share from the beginning
to end—and planning the trip
is part of the beginning—it's a
disaster. I won't do all the planning by myself. And even if I
did, it wouldn't work. You
would not have agreed to do
any of the chores that need
doing. It wouldn't work.

RAFAEL: Well, I want to go. I
ain't never been to no big park
like that.

CORKY: Cool it, man. Hey, Mr.
Hank, are you one of those anti-
pot types?

Corky, ever testing Hank, tries
to put him on the defensive.

HANK: I can't say I like it,
Corky. But in this case, it's not a
question of whether I like it.
Look, let me ask you something.
We were supposed to make plans
at our last meeting. Can you tell
me one decision we made?

Hank does not get side-tracked
in a discussion of the pros and
cons of marijuana. Instead he
sticks to reality—pot and planning do not mix. To make his
point, he asks the group to cite
any decision about the trip
made during last week's meeting, hoping this will help them
see that no progress was made.

DENNY: [Grumbling.] I can't
see what's wrong with having a
little fun.

HANK: Denny, you're not
hearin' me. There's nothing

Hank picks up Denny's point to
delineate the difference between

wrong with having fun. But—well—look, last meeting you had fun, right?

DENNY: Fun. Yeah, fun.

HANK: And what did we decide about the trip at the meeting?

RAFAEL: That we wanted to go, man!

THOMAS: Ah, we did that 2 weeks ago! Where was you last week? Last week we didn't do nothing, man, except crack up about my gorgeous nose.

CORKY: Cyrano de Boop-a-crack!

HANK: Well—and if you guys blow pot in town—when we're trying to plan the trip—well, what's to say you won't be getting high in camp when there are jobs to be done: You know, jobs in camp are fun, too—just 'cause you are in camp. But if you're high, chances are they won't get done and the whole trip will be a mess.

DENNY: You mean no pot in camp?

HANK: Well, do you think camp will work out if you guys are all the time blasting?

having fun and having fun at the right time.

Thomas is beginning to appreciate the group's problem.

Denny is finally realizing the implications of Hank's confrontation.

Hank wants to avoid setting a limit he knows he will be unable to enforce. He hopes that his use of Confrontation will lead the group to set this limit on themselves.

As the discussion continues, Hank knows that the boys must resolve this dilemma before he will take them to camp. Otherwise, he is sure that it will be a disaster. He wonders if he proposed this trip before the group was ready to handle it. There is enough motivation to go, however, and enough trust of Hank among the boys that the group's development may be enhanced by having to face this issue.

In this example, a group Leader has confronted a group: The same principles would apply when a Leader confronts an individual (except that the Leader may then be in a better position to draw on group members to do the confronting), or when members of a group confront one another, or when the group confronts its Leader.

EXERCISE

Goals

When participating in a group, you should be able to recognize when an inconsistency in behavior calls for confrontation. Verbally confront that inconsistency in such a way that the other members say that they recognize the inconsistency and agree to behave in a way that is consistent with the group's contract. The purpose of this exercise is to:

1. practice Confrontation;
2. experience Confrontation;
3. give you some feedback from others about your use (within the group) of the techniques covered to date; that is, are you seen as Attending well to other participants, do you give information clearly, have you Rewarded others in the learning group appropriately, and so on?

Materials

1. Ballpoint pens or pencils of the same color, and enough 3-x-5 cards for each member to have two separate cards for every other member of the group, including him- or herself. For example, in a group of nine, each member would have 18 cards, so that a total of 162 cards would be needed for the entire group.
2. Chairs arranged in a circle.

Process

Phase I. Pass out the cards and ballpoint pens or pencils. At the top of each card, write the name of each group member, followed by the Roman numeral I until you have a separate card for each participant, including yourself. Now make a second set of cards in the same way for Phase II; next to each name write Roman numeral II.

On the Phase I set of cards for each person, including your own, write the name of the technique he or she uses best and your reasons for thinking so.[1] If possible, refer to an example from a recent meeting. *Technique* refers to the one that you think the member uses in such a way that the group's or the individual's goals (as stated in your contract) are more likely to be reached. (Remember to include yourself.) In writing this statement, members are to write so that it would be impossible to identify the author of the statement (which is why everybody uses the same color ballpoint pen). Please confine your writing to one side of the card.

Using the second set of cards, name the technique that the participant uses least effectively and write a brief statement (a few sentences) that describes his or her use of this technique. *Uses least effectively* means the way in which the member's use of the technique makes it less likely that the group's or the member's goals will be achieved. You can think of this as the "needs most improvement" card. (Remember to include a card for yourself.) Again, write this statement so that it is not possible to identify the author of the statement. Turn these cards face down in front of you.

In any way you choose, select one participant. We will call that member "X." Have everyone in turn (going clockwise around the circle) read out loud from the Phase I card what they have written about X. Finally, X should read what he or she has written about himself or herself. Now repeat this procedure for every participant of the group until all Phase I cards have been read for each participant.

Phase II. Everyone should now pass (face down) their Phase II card *about the first X to the member seated to X's left:* that member is designated C (for confronter). C then shuffles the cards, face down.

X now tells the group what he or she anticipates the "needs most improvement" feedback will be. C then reads what each person has written about X. Because the cards have been shuffled, it should not be possible to identify the authors of these statements. (Destroying these cards after this exercise will preserve this anonymity.)

Once all comments have been read about X, he or she is given the opportunity to respond.

C should mentally compare what has been written about X with X's comments about what he or she expected people would say as well as his or her response to the written statements. If there is a discrepancy, C must confront X with it and attempt a resolution with X. If C thinks it appropriate, he or she may invite the group to join in confronting X.

After a few minutes, stop the discussion and *review C's use of Confrontation.*

Now repeat the procedure as follows: C becomes the new X, the person to his or her left becomes the next C, and so on around the circle going through Phase II for each person as time will allow.

POSTSCRIPT: ISSUES IN CONFRONTATION

The major theoretical support for the use of Confrontation comes from Festinger's (1957) theory of *cognitive dissonance* (Brehm & Cohen, 1962). This theory is based on the following three assumptions:

1. Attitude or opinion change follows behavioral change.
2. Dissonance (defined as a significant discrepancy between two of an individual's cognitions) is experienced as a tension-producing condition by that individual.
3. A person who is experiencing dissonance will try to resolve the discrepancy that has caused the dissonance, thus reducing his or her discomfort.

Festinger and Aronson (1968) suggest the following example of dissonance: A person believes that the Democratic presidential candidate is the best person for the job but votes for the Republican out of social pressure or family tradition. The cognition that the Democrat is more qualified is dissonant with the individual's cognition about voting Republican. (It is important to note that the dissonance is not simply between cognitions [i.e., ideas or attitudes] but the behavior associated with these cognitions as well.) Cognitive dissonance theory suggests that our Republican-voting friend is most likely to resolve the discrepancy (i.e., reduce the dissonance) in one of the following ways:

1. Change behavior, attitudes, or ideas so that the dissonance is diminished. This might be done by subscribing to a newspaper that favors Republican candidates and presents them in the best light, associating with Republicans rather than Democrats, searching for subtle wisdom in the speeches of Republican candidates, and so forth.
2. Try to discredit the source of the dissonant information or ignore it altogether; for example, stop reading reports of speeches by Democrats, search for evidence of faults in Democratic candidates, and so on.
3. Discredit the importance of his or her own behavior; for example, decide that his or her vote really had no effect on the outcome of the election.

Effective Confrontation seeks to have the individual change attitudes, ideas, and behaviors, rather than try to hold onto old ways through discrediting others or discounting the importance of one's own behaviors.

One weakness in the theory is the notion that individuals experience tension (caused by discrepancies in thoughts and/or action) to be so uncomfortable that they feel they must eliminate the discrepancies. This assumption is questionable: Some people seem to thrive on tension and pressure. This suggests the need to choose the issue being confronted with great care so that the individual is forced to confront the reality that the discrepancy, unless resolved, will prove costly for him or her. For example, "You say you want a job, and indeed you've worked very hard to be ready for one. Yet you show up for this critical job interview, smelling of booze, sloppily dressed, and generally higher than a kite." Assuming the individual *has* chosen to work toward finding a job, and assuming that he or she is unable to justifiably accuse the confronter with a history of downgrading statements, the person is left in conflict, which is precisely where this theory suggests you want him or her to be.

IN PREPARATION

In the next chapter there is an exercise in which you are asked to teach someone to do something by demonstrating it to them. If you plan to use this exercise, you should select something you can teach in 5 to 10 minutes and plan to bring whatever equipment you need to the Modeling session. For example, if you were going to teach someone how to knit, you would bring knitting needles and yarn sufficient for you and several others. Whatever you select should be "do-able" within the limitations of equipment and time. Other possibilities: how to do a particular card trick, how to tie a bowtie, how to speak a few key phrases in a language other than English.

NOTE

1. Choose from the chapters you've covered so far (Attending, Information Seeking, Information Giving, Contract Negotiation, Rewarding, Responding to Feeling, Focusing, Summarizing, and Gatekeeping).

SUGGESTED READINGS

Chandler, L. (1979). Cognitive dissonance in the parent conference. *Elementary School Guidance and Counseling, 14*(1), 12-15.

Egan, G. (1976). Confrontation. *Group and Organization Studies, 1*(2), 223-243.

Festinger, L. (1962). *A theory of cognitive dissonance*. Stanford, CA: Stanford University Press.

Fink, D. (1992). The psychotherapy of multiple personality disorder: A case study. *Psychoanalytic Inquiry, 12*(1), 49-70.

Goldberg, R., & Wise, T. (1985). Psychodynamic strategies for telephone scatology. *American Journal of Psychoanalysis, 45*(3), 291-297.

Hazam, Y., Lerner, Y., & Subar, R. (1992). Coping with acting-out in a psychoanalytically-oriented adolescent unit. *British Journal of Psychotherapy, 8*(4), 359-373.

Littrell, J., & Magel, D. (1991). The influence of self-concept on change in client behaviors: A review. *Research in Social Work Practice, 1*(1), 46-67.

Milgram, D., & Rubin, J. (1992). Resisting resistance: Involuntary substance abuse group therapy. *Social Work With Groups, 15*(1), 95-110.

Purpura, P. (1985). The use of confrontation in the treatment of narcissistic and masochistic character resistances. *Issues in Ego Psychology, 8*(1-2), 48-51.

Scavo, R., & Buchanan, B. (1989). Group therapy for male adolescent sex offenders: A model for residential treatment. *Residential Treatment for Children and Youth, 7*(2), 59-74.

Ulrich, J. (1991). A motivational approach to the treatment of alcoholism in the Federal Republic of Germany. *Alcoholism Treatment Quarterly, 8*(2), 83-92.

Chapter 11

MODELING

HOW DO YOU DESCRIBE MODELING?

Modeling occurs when a participant in a group demonstrates a behavior or set of behaviors in such a way that another person can imitate it. The demonstrator is called the "model"; the imitator is called the "learner." For example, John tells the group that he always mishandled the part of the job interview that dealt with his arrest record. Bill, another member, knows that Pete has developed a good approach to this problem and suggests that Pete show John how to handle it. In the role play that follows, Bill plays a friendly employer and Pete plays himself, showing how he handles questions about his prior arrests. Then John takes Pete's role in a rerun of the skit and tries to approximate his performance. Both Pete and the rest of the group then tell John how he did, first praising his attempt, then suggesting some improvements. John tries it again and does better. Someone rewards him for this improvement, *then* suggests a further improvement. Then a member plays a hostile employer and John tries once again; as before, the group provides feedback about his performance, first rewarding the improvements. This entire process is made possible by John's Modeling of an effective way to describe one's arrest history during a job interview.

What is an example of Modeling that you have seen recently?

_____

_____

_____

WHEN DO YOU USE MODELING?

1. When a leader and some members (a) understand what action creates difficulties for other participants and (b) are reasonably certain that there are substitute things to say or do that can be shown to them and that are likely to improve the situation.

2. When participants are behaving toward one another in ways that are destructive or unhelpful, and you want them to learn new ways of interacting or remind them of social skills they already have, but are not using in this situation.

3. When members' behaviors are not totally ineffective, but could be considerably better.

4. When members need to develop more than one way of responding effectively to a situation that is problematic for them as individuals or in a group.

In the example of Modeling that you have described, was it used at the appropriate time? Why do you think so?

_____

_____

_____

HOW DO YOU USE MODELING?

To obtain the best results,[1] follow these steps in order:

1. Determine that the learner wants to learn from the model; that is, *work out a modeling contract.*

2. Have the model *demonstrate* to show the learner how to do something.

3. Have the learner attempt to *imitate* the demonstrator: initially, as exact of a word-for-word, action-for-action imitation as possible, until the learner feels comfortable using his or her own words and actions.

4. Provide the learner with *feedback,* telling how well he or she did. Be sure to give praise for correct parts of his or her performance *first,* before you suggest improvements.

5. The learner should *practice* the behavior, making corrections as needed, and then *improvise* the behavior to fit conditions different from those in the original demonstration; as above when John, in imitating Pete, was first confronted with a "friendly employer," just as Pete had been, and then was forced to improvise in coping with a "hostile employer."

Selecting the best model is important. The model should be someone who can perform the behavior correctly, is important to the learner, is clearly visible to the learner, and is sufficiently like the learner so that the learner believes that he or she could, in time, do as well as the model. The Leader is not the only possible model; indeed, it is sometimes preferable to use a group member as the model. *Former* members could also be drawn in as models, assuming they have achieved some improvement in terms of problematic behavior.

It is essential that the learner be taught to *recognize the same cues* to which the model responded. For example, the cue that Pete said led him to discuss his arrest record was that the interview had been underway for about 5 minutes with no questions having been asked about a police record; he tried to anticipate rather than wait for a question about his record. He explained that interviewers were usually impressed with his honesty and his desire to prove that he could do well; if this information turned them off, it was best to know early in the interview, so as to avoid the problems that would follow the discovery of his arrest record. Some of the members disagreed with Pete, saying it was better to conceal a record, but it was at least clear to John *why* Pete did what he did and why he did it at that particular point in the interview.

When the behavior to be learned is fairly complex, slow down the demonstration, or *break it up*, working on one piece at a time. But be sure that the learner eventually practices the *entire performance* at a normal pace.

If a learner is attempting to copy the demonstration in front of the group, you should make it possible (if he or she wishes) for him or her to first practice the behavior in private (perhaps off in a corner) mentally rehearsing what he or she will say. Let the learner tell you when he or she is ready perform in front of others. Be sure to arrange the practice so that it comes as *close as possible to the real situation* in which the modeled behavior is to be used. As noted above, it is important to *reward the learner* for those portions of his or her approximation that are correct. Also, be sure to reward the *model* in the presence of the learner. This will increase the likelihood that the learner will imitate the model.

Sometimes, when you are attempting to serve as a model for "good group participation behaviors," you may not always want to call direct attention to yourself. For example, you would probably not say, "Now watch how I step in to use Gatekeeping with our overtalkative members." On the other hand, you should be sure to *reward participants who imitate your "good group participation behaviors"* whenever they emulate the behavior you want them to acquire. In addition, reward members who are models of good group behavior, so that the other participants are helped to recognize good group participation in action. Research has shown that rewarding a *model* increases the probability that others will emulate him or her.

In the example of Modeling that you described, was it used effectively? Why?

_____

_____

_____

HOW DO YOU KNOW YOU HAVE
USED MODELING SUCCESSFULLY?

1. In a previously problematic situation, the participants change their behavior enough so that the problem is sufficiently resolved for them to achieve their goals. They do this by first imitating the model to some degree and then adapting whatever they have imitated to their own way of doing things.

2. Individuals will imitate your behavior (or the behavior of other members) to a greater and greater degree, and do so in such a way that progress toward individual and group goals is furthered for most (if not all) participants.

OPPRESSION AND EMPOWERMENT
IN RELATION TO MODELING

It often has been observed that individuals who see themselves as members of an oppressed population can, over time, come to accept the negative image others have of them. When this happens, minority group members (for example) can develop a sour view of themselves, with little hope of ever being anything better. One way to overcome this kind of pessimism is to facilitate interactions with members of that minority group who *have* escaped the bonds of oppression. Nowadays, for example, it is common to see television ads of famous African-American professional athletes, encouraging adolescents to stay in school and stay off drugs. Although these ads probably have their value, it has to be recognized that these same youngsters are not stupid: they know that only a tiny fraction of kids like themselves are likely to become millionaire athletes. To be effective, a role model has to be doing better than the "modelee," but also has to be sufficiently like the modelee for that person to believe they have a real chance to match the model's successful performance. A far better model is someone from the neighborhood who *did* stay in school and is now in the middle of his or her college education. Clients in a substance abuse program can benefit greatly from seeing someone just a few years older than themselves—a member of the same minority group with which they identify—who has been "clean" for the past 3 years and now has a decent and interesting job with good possibilities for advancement. In some cases, it can even make sense for a human services program to invite back one of its former clients to be a group member, sharing his or her day-by-day experiences with slow and sometimes faltering, but generally steady success. Another approach is for programs to hire their own graduates—those who show the greatest promise—to work in the program as a model of successful accomplishment. The bottom line is that the models have to be believable, so that the "modelee" can think, "If *she* can make it, so can I!"

Of course, there is more to effective Modeling (and that is described in this chapter), but without selecting and highlighting the actions of *believable* models, the rest of the process is not likely to work.

AN EXAMPLE OF MODELING

SCENE

Cottage Five, on E Wing, at the State Training School for boys, holds regular weekly meetings to discuss any problems the boys may be having. There are 10 boys in the cottage ranging in age from 14 to 17. All of the boys have been in this cottage at least 3 months; Pete, the "senior citizen," is in his 11th month at the School. The boys are sent to the School from juvenile courts all around the state. Their backgrounds include a variety of offenses such as car theft and breaking and entering. Half of the boys in Cottage Five are black.

Mr. Archer: The Wing Man who is in charge of the meeting has been a staff member at the school for the past 4 years. He is black.

Pete: The boy who has been at the school longer than any boy in the cottage (11 months) and the unofficial leader of the group; 17 years old, black.

Duck: So called because of his funny walk; a fast talker and "con" artist; 15 years old, white

Ron: The boy with a problem, which is his relationship with his math teacher; 14 years old, black.

Arthur: A "cool dude," next in line to Pete in both age (16) and length of stay (10 months), black

Sam: 15, white, a good student in the classroom

Spider: 15, white

Victor: 16, black

T. J.: 14, black

Arnold: 16, white

Finn: 14, white

Up to this point, the meeting has dealt with cottage problems. Prior to the meeting, Ron had told Mr. Archer that he wanted the group's help.

ACTION	DISCUSSION
MR. ARCHER: Ron has asked for some group time. Ron?	Archer knows what the problem is, but wants Ron to present it to the group.
RON: [Embarrassed, but determined] Yeah—well, see—I—well, well, it's—uh—my math class. Like, I'm messin' up.	Ron asks for help but does so in a vague way.
Pete: Speak up, boy! What you mean, messin' up? Be spee-cific!	Pete has been in group meetings often enough to understand the staff's emphasis on behavioral specificity.
RON: Like—uh—the teacher is all the time buggin' me, you know, 'cause I can't get nothin' right. And the more, you know, I try, the worse it gets, 'til after a while I don't even know my—my own name, know what I mean?	Ron describes his concern with more clarity.
ARTHUR: Well, look here, do you ask the teacher for help? Who is it—Spitz?	Arthur bores right in. He knows how confusing math can be.
RON: Yeah, Spitz.	
ARTHUR: Well, do you ask him for help?	

RON: Well, you know, he says I gotta think about it and—and I try, but . . .

PETE: Yeah, but, like the man says, do you ask ol' Spitzy for help? He's a straight stud. He'll help if you ask.

ARTHUR: That's right. He helped me.

RON: Yeah—well—but I mean—well, I guess I just don't know how.

The real problem becomes clear: Ron does not know how to ask for help when he needs it.

MR. ARCHER: Hey, I got an idea. Arthur, you say you had a good experience in getting help from Mr. Spitz. Why don't you show Ron how to do it? We'll make Duck here be Mr. Spitz. OK, Duck? You know him?

Archer has kept quiet, allowing the group to bring the problem into focus. Now he suggests a role play in which Arthur (who he knows has good relationships with adults) will demonstrate how to ask an adult for help. He brings in Duck because it's been difficult to get him involved in the group's discussions.

DUCK: [Grins, puffs out his chest, grabs a pencil from the table and puts it behind his ear. Screws up his face so that he looks very serious.] Sure!

PETE: [Laughs.] Looks just like the dude!

Mr. Archer is surprised and delighted that he has apparently found a way to involve Duck.

MR. ARCHER: Great, Duck! OK, Ron, Arthur here is going to show you how to get Mr. Spitz's help. Watch what he does 'cause I'm gonna ask you to do the same thing, just for practice, in a minute. OK?

Archer briefly describes the process as it will occur. It is quick contracting, but the group has used role playing before, so he can assume the process he is introducing will be understood.

RON: OK. I'll try it.

Ron agrees to the contract.

MR. ARCHER: OK, Duck. Why don't you sit over there at the head of the table?

Archer sets the scene.

PETE: Yeah, and he be grading some papers. Give him those papers, man.

Pete gets into the spirit of the role play.

MR. ARCHER: Ready, Duck? Arthur? OK. Go!

DUCK: [Studiously grading papers and exclaiming over them to himself as he does so—he's really feeling the part.] Splendid student! Obviously a superior mind. That boy deserves an A plus! But this one! No hope, no hope. Must be one of the boys from D wing. Hopeless. Oh. Yes, Arthur?

Duck horses around a bit but nevertheless provides a good version of Mr. Spitz for Arthur's demonstration.

ARTHUR: [Has walked over to Duck's desk. Pausing momentarily, waiting until Duck notices him.] Excuse me, Mr. Spitz, I'm having trouble with problem nine. Would you have a minute to show me how to do it?

The demonstration.

MR. ARCHER: Cut! Great Arthur, just great. OK, Ron, why don't you try it?

Archer cuts it short—just enough to show Ron how to get started. Note, too, his praise of Arthur's demonstration. This is an important part of the process.

RON: Yeah. OK.

DUCK: [Back in his part again and enjoying it. Mumbling to himself as he again grades papers.] Don't know what I'm going to do with those dummies in D wing. Haven't an ounce of sense—oh. Yes, Ron?

RON: Uh, Mr.—uh—Spitz. Excuse me. I'm having trouble with number nine. Could you do it for me?

Ron tries an imitation. Not bad for a first try, but he makes a mistake. He asks Mr. Spitz to do it for him, whereas Arthur had asked, "Would you have a minute to show me how to do it?"

MR. ARCHER: Cut. Good Ron. That was a good beginning. Arthur?

Archer cuts it short again, praises the attempt, then asks Arthur for feedback.

ARTHUR: Yeah, that was cool. But, look man, don't ask the dude to do nothin' for you 'cause he never will. See, the grown-ups around here—they don't like to do nothin' for you.

Arthur also first praises Ron. [Is he perhaps imitating Mr. Archer's modeling of a "positive" approach?] Then he points out Ron's error.

Archer notes this little byplay between Pete and Arthur. He knows it for what it is—friendly teasing of himself—and lets it slide.

PETE: Why, what ever are you saying, my good man?

ARTHUR: Yeah, well, I said it. I mean, Ron, ask him to "show you how," you dig?

MR. ARCHER: OK, thanks Arthur, that's a good point. Clear, Ron?

Archer praises Arthur and underscores his point in the process.

RON: Um-hmm.

MR. ARCHER: Fine. Now let's try it again and remember to ask him to show you how to do it, not to do it for you. Ready?

Archer sets up a second attempt by Ron.

Ron tried a second time and did so well that the whole group applauded his performance. Mr. Archer then asked Duck to be less helpful and then had Ron try to approach him when he did not respond quite so sympathetically. Eventually, Ron said he thought he could ask the math teacher for help and promised to report back to the group on his efforts to do so at their next meeting.

EXERCISE

Goals

When participating in a group, you should be able to recognize when Modeling could prove useful, then follow the six step process—contract, demonstrate, imitate, feedback, practice, and improvise—so that imitation of the desired behavior(s) occurs.

Time Required

Variable.

Specialized Roles

Some members will be models, others will be learners.

Process

Members should have selected an activity in which they have enough skill to serve as a model, as described at the end of Chapter 10. You can learn a great deal about Modeling and have an enjoyable session by selecting activities that are interesting and fun for the members of this group.

Although all members should prepare (and thus have the experience of planning a demonstration), you may want only one or two members (two would be better for contrast) to serve as models, with the rest of the group as learners. Or you can break into pairs or small groups and have each member model to the others in his or her subgroup. If you choose this route, you could first have each person announce what he or she plans to model and then allow the members to vote on the demonstration subject(s) that interest them most. Then form subgroups around the people teaching those activities. This would give you an opportunity to experience the effect of an individual's motivation on the way in which he or she learns from a model.

In any event, reserve time to discuss your experience. Be sure when doing this to compare your experiences with the suggested six-step process. In your discussion, devote some attention to the use of Modeling in your work; for example, who could serve as models, how you could arrange to reward models in the presence of learners, and so on.

POSTSCRIPT: ISSUES IN MODELING

Years ago, many human service professionals gave up on alcoholics. In response to these, a few alcoholics—searching for a way to get help with their addiction—created a new form of group work: the support group. Known as Alcoholics Anonymous, this group approach was designed to operate *without* the guidance of trained professionals, and it became the model for support groups of all kinds. Several years ago, one of my students did a survey of support groups operating in the Ann Arbor community, and she identified 35 *different* populations that were participating in their own specialized support groups. I mentioned her survey to one of my other students, who then informed me of another that was not on the list of 35. This was a group she had recently helped to start in our community: the Endometriosis Association. The success of the support group approach is due, in part, to its low cost; but more important, to the availability in support groups of viable models who inspire potential members with the hope that this program can work for them!

In a support group, individuals who share common problems with others describe their experiences with that problem and do so in a believable way. In doing so, they play out the notion that people are more likely to model the behavior of someone they perceive to be similar to themselves, yet who is performing more effectively than they are. It is this similarity that plants the idea, "If he or she can do it, perhaps I can, too!" The implication of the "similarity factor" lies in the process of group composition. Rather than just putting anyone in a group to fill it up, you should try to compose your group with members who have mixed abilities (with regard to the problem that has brought them together) so that members can serve as models for one another (see Bertcher & Maple, 1977, pp. 19-22). That means that you have to know something about each potential member—the more the better—when you are composing your group (assuming you have the authority to decide who will or will not be in the group). In addition to using group composition as a way of "seeding" a group with potential models, you need to pay attention to what members say and do once the group begins. You may discover that member X is a good model for others in the group when it comes to a particular problem because X has already dealt effectively with that problem, and this may be a fact of which you were unaware when the group began.

IN PREPARATION

The exercise for Mediating involves two role plays for which background information and "get-you-started" scripts are provided. It would be useful to photocopy the scripts, separating the printouts in such a way that each participant receives only one script: the appropriate one for their own role.

NOTE

1. People continually learn from one another through modeling (i.e., copying someone else's behavior) whether or not they have contracted to do so. Sometimes, all you can hope to do is behave in a way that you hope others will want to emulate. Contracting for learning via Modeling, however, increases the probability that the desired learning will occur.

SUGGESTED READINGS

Baldwin, T. (1992). Effects of alternative modeling strategies on outcomes of interpersonal-skills training. *Journal of Applied Psychology, 77*(2),147-154.

Bandura, W. (1986). *Social foundations of thought and action: A social cognitive theory.* Englewood Cliffs, NJ: Prentice Hall.

Bertcher, H. (1973). The child care worker as a role model. *Child Care Quarterly, 2*(3), 178-191.

Bertcher, H. (1978). Guidelines for the group worker's use of role modeling. *Social Work With Groups, 1*(3),233-246.

Borgers, S., & Koenig, R. (1983). Uses and effects of modeling by the therapist in group therapy. *Journal for Specialists in Group Work, 8*(3), 133-138.

Owens, C., & Ascione, F. (1991). Effects of the model's age, perceived similarity, and familiarization on children's donating. *Journal of Genetic Psychology, 152*(3), 341-357.

Rose, S. (1990). Putting the group into cognitive-behavioral treatment. *Social Work With Groups, 13*(3), 71-83.

Wyrwicka, W. (1988). Imitative behavior: A theoretical view. *Pavlovian Journal of Biological Science, 23*(3), 125-131.

Chapter 12

MEDIATING

HOW DO YOU DESCRIBE MEDIATING?

Mediating involves putting oneself in a neutral position between opponents in order to avoid or resolve a disagreement that is keeping the group from reaching its goals.

What is an example of Mediating that you have seen recently?

_____

_____

_____

WHEN DO YOU USE MEDIATING?

Disagreement and conflict are natural in any group and are often quite productive. They can also interfere with the group's work when opinions become polarized, when interaction becomes more emotional than rational, and when impasses occur. When a difference of opinion is (or appears likely to be) of sufficient duration or intensity to disrupt the group's work on its contracted goals, Mediating can be used. Specific behaviors to watch for include the following: members stop trying to understand one another and, instead, champion their own causes without Attending to others; voices are raised; people look strained, turn away, or push back from the table as if to escape from the group; an argument continues for some time with no resolution.

Mediating is used when an unresolved conflict exists in the group. In order to recognize the point at which Mediating is required, you need to have some idea of the normal level of conflict that can be handled comfortably by group members. In other words, the better you know your group, the more likely it is that you will be able to use Mediating on time, rather than jumping in too early (which stops a potentially useful exchange) or intervening so late that irreparable damage occurs (e.g., members decide that it is impossible to get anything useful from this group and quit or withdraw from the interaction).

In regard to the example of Mediating that you have described, was it used at the appropriate time? Why do you think so?

_____

_____

_____

HOW DO YOU MEDIATE?

Build a Reputation for Fairness

The successful Mediator is someone who is viewed as fair by all parties concerned. This kind of reputation can be earned over time by Attending equally to different points of view and by discussing controversial issues without being trapped into an aggressive defense or offense on behalf of one point of view. You may certainly have your own opinion and you may even state it, but you do so in a way that shows you recognize that others may see things differently and can come to their own conclusions.

Encourage Group Members to Mediate

If you are the Leader, you should allow a period of time for group members to attempt to play this role before you try to Mediate. If they react to the controversy by drawing back as if to say, "You're the Leader, you handle it," you should ask yourself if the group members can handle this situation. If they can, encourage them to do so; if not, you may have to use Mediating yourself. In that case, you should take the initiative and firmly call a halt to the conflict.

If you are not the group's Leader but are a member and do not wish to do the Mediating yourself, you could ask other participants to step in; for example, "Joe, you're pretty good at straightening out disagreements. Don't you think you could help Mary and Pete resolve their differences here?"

Clarify the Issues

Ask the opponents to restate their positions as clearly as they can; if this does not work—that is, if it does not make clear what issues are at stake and how the two points of view differ—ask other participants to state the two positions as they understand them. A different tack is to ask the opponents to restate the other person's point of view. It is essential that proponents of a point of view confirm that a fair statement of their positions has been made when stated by someone other than its proponent.

Invoke Positive Elements

Mediating can be done by appealing to group harmony, group goals, old friendships, or anything related to the group's contract that will remind the combatants of the positive tie between them. In this vein, humor is often useful for purposes of "tension decontamination." [1]

Suggested Steps in Mediating

Move next to a proposed resolution. The following are good examples:

- Search for more information on which to make a choice.
- Look for a compromise position.
- Ask for a vote to determine whether or not there is a clear majority position.
- Agree, if you cannot reach a mutually acceptable position, to temporarily set aside the issue until the discussion is less heated.
- Suggest that members be allowed to maintain their own position—that is, agree to disagree.
- Suggest that those who are disagreeing go up the values hierarchy of the group until a value or norm on which everyone can agree is found; for example, "Well, maybe you can't agree on this point, but we agreed that we're to be finished with this report by the end of the month. Unless we work this out now, we'll never make it."

Mediating and the Contract

When one position appears to be consistent with the contract and the other is in violation of the contract, it may be necessary to take the risk of supporting the procontract position or of renegotiating the contract when members are less upset. The risk is that you may resolve the issue at the cost of alienating one or more members. If it is a question of group survival, there may be no choice. Hopefully, the group will have used other approaches successfully so that it will not reach this point. Alienated participants might quit on the spot—always a jolt for those who stay behind—or they may stay, harboring a strong resentment about the fact that some people "took sides" against them.

What Happens if There Is a Loser?

If there is a decision in which one point of view "loses," particular attention should be paid to the response of the "defeated party." Members may quit or withdraw from their normal level of participation in the group. If this happens, an extra effort may need to be made to reinvolve such persons in the activities of the group by such methods as Gatekeeping in their favor, Attending to them, Focusing on and Rewarding their contribution, and so on.

In regard to the example of Mediating that you have described, was it used effectively? Why?

HOW DO YOU KNOW THAT MEDIATING HAS BEEN USED SUCCESSFULLY?

Tension associated with the difference of opinion is eased and the issue is decided through compromise or is temporarily set aside. Setting the conflict aside may be achieved (a) by an agreement to disagree, (b) by scheduling a "rehearing" on the controversial topic when members can be less emotional or when information that has been lacking becomes available to the group, or (c) by renegotiating the contract. Indications that the conflict has been settled include the following: members resume Attending to one another, discussion continues without raised voices, participants propose compromises that are accepted, members sit in relaxed positions, members joke about their disagreement in a friendly way, and so on.

OPPRESSION AND EMPOWERMENT IN RELATION TO MEDIATING

In a group whose members represent different populations, at least one of which is oppressed, there are likely to be conflicts as that group interacts and develops over time. Some of these conflicts are bound to reflect differences associated with prejudice and discrimination related to population identity. When this occurs, the group worker may find him- or herself trying to work out the differences between members in ways that will settle the immediate issues, while at the same time trying to establish a set of group norms that would facilitate the settling of such conflicts in the future.

This may involve the use of skillful mediating, in which the group worker is seen by all as a neutral third party: Someone who is only interested in a fair and mutually accepted settlement of the conflict.

But suppose the group Leader is also a member of one of the populations that is involved in the conflict. For example, in an African-American/Caucasian mixed group, suppose the Leader is Caucasian. If the conflict is heated, a Caucasian Leader might be viewed by the African-American members as biased, simply because of his or her race. In such a case, it may be very difficult for the Leader to be seen as a fair, impartial mediator. If and when this happens, there are several ways of dealing with it:

1. The Leader can simply tough it out, demonstrating in word and deed his or her essential fairness and desire to see the matter settled fairly and to everyone's satisfaction.

2. The Leader could decide to recognize, with the group, that some might question his or her ability to be impartial and offer to step aside as a potential mediator, bringing in an outside mediator who is knowledgeable in the role of mediator, but who clearly is from neither of the "warring" populations (e.g., in the situation referred to above, an Asian-American woman).

3. The Leader might recognize, with the group, the need for mediation, accompanied by the group's suspicion that the Leader cannot be counted on to be fair in helping settle the issue. He or she can then negotiate a process in which group members from each population attempt to serve as *Co*mediators working together toward conflict resolution, with the Leader on the sidelines as an available consultant.

Given these three possibilities, it seems more likely that effective mediation could occur and that the conflict could be resolved in a way that is acceptable to everyone.

AN EXAMPLE OF MEDIATING

SCENE

In an effort to develop a closer tie between the community and the juvenile court, Judge Randolph (of that court) created a citizens-advisory committee. The attempt was to involve a cross section of the community, with a mix of interested citizens and professionals whose agencies had dealings with the court. At most meetings, three members of the court staff attended to give information and interpret the court's philosophy. Occasionally, when his schedule permits, the judge sits in, although he usually leaves midway through the meeting because of the conflicting demands on his time.

The committee is composed of the following persons:

Pat Nijeski: Pediatrician's nurse, chairwoman
Ralph Dixon: Gas station owner
Phil Bolt: Department store manager
Dr. Peter Grant: University faculty member
Martha Greenberg: Welfare department supervisor
William Hale: Community center director
Corinne Malm: Child guidance-clinic social worker
Bob Lopez: Runaway center worker
Diane Wilkmore: High school guidance counselor
Burt Schwartz: Administrative director of the juvenile court
Lisa McGinnis: Head of the probation department of the court
Thurmond Lee: Head of the intake department of the court

The committee meets once a month at the court. Because it has been formed only recently, its members have asked for considerable orientation to the activities of the court. Just prior to this meeting, Corinne, Bob, and Diane visited the detention facility run by the court. At the point in the meeting at which the script begins, Bob is giving the group's report of their visit. His tone is sharp and critical.

ACTION	DISCUSSION
BOB: [Speaking rapidly.] So there are 15 kids there and we talked to about half of them. Half, Diane?	Bob is angry, and he does not care who knows it (or what effect it has on the group).
DIANE: Six, to be exact, Bob.	
BOB: Six. OK. Well, almost half. [Shakes his head.] Boy, it's a mess. I don't know where to begin. Those kids had a list of grievances a mile long. Sleeping	

area too crowded, toilet dirty
and needing repair, showers
don't work, no constructive
recreation—

PAT: Slow down, Bob, I'm not
following—you're talking too
fast. Just what's got you so upset?

Pat sees trouble ahead and tries
to assert some control, but with
little success.

BOB: Upset? Mad is more like.
I wouldn't have believed that we
treat kids like that!

BURT: [Obviously annoyed but
trying to be patient.] Could you
be more specific?

Burt is responsible for the management of the detention facility. He knows it is not adequate
and is hoping that this committee will help to focus attention
on his program's needs, but he
is annoyed by Bob's irritating
manner.

BOB: You bet I can! For example, according to my notes—
lemme see here—OK—yeah.
Discipline. Now sure, maybe the
kids were just pulling our legs.
But one thing they've got up
there is this beat up old pool
table.

BURT: [Under his breath.] Beat
up is right! Wish we could afford a new one.

A *sotto voce* comment that Bob
misses.

BOB: [Didn't hear.] OK. Well, the
kids say that if you drop a pool ball
on the floor, no matter what the reason, that's 10 push-ups!

WILLIAM: The way I play pool
I'd be doing a lot of push-ups.

William is trying to use humor
to soften the growing conflict,
but it does not work.

BOB: Yeah, but push-ups? No
matter why the ball fell? Even if
it was an accident?

BURT: Well, that happens to be the way it is! Look, we get all kinds of kids there, from all over the county, most of them for a short period of time. Control is a very real problem. So we have to run a pretty tight ship!

Burt is really annoyed at Bob's total failure to understand the explosive situation they face in detention. Nevertheless, he tries to explain their rationale.

BOB: Yeah, but that's like a lousy marine drill station! It's ridiculous!

Bob bores right in with the accusations.

BURT: You wouldn't think it's so ridiculous if you had to pull regular shifts over there—day in and day out—'specially when we're so understaffed. The way we do it, nobody gets out of line. Look, detention isn't treatment, we're simply holding them until—

Bob is not mad at Burt, but Burt is mad at Bob. And the conflict escalates another notch.

BOB: And that's another thing! One kid told me he'd been there for 5 months. Five months! Now you can't tell me that's detention.

Now Bob is off on another grievance and no one, with the exception of William, has tried to deal with the argument. William's attempt failed because it had nothing to do with the substance of the dispute.

THURMOND: It so happens I know that boy's situation well. And that's one we've been pushing the welfare department on—to come up with foster homes so we can move kids out. But, we just get the royal run-around!

The hot feelings are contagious. Now Thurmond is responding in a highly defensive manner and, in a minute, will draw Martha into this angry whirlpool.

MARTHA: Now, wait a minute, Thurmond, if you're talking about that Ganker's case you know full well that—

Martha feels called on to defend her territory.

PAT: Whoa! Hold it! Boy, I'm gonna need a referee's whistle in a minute. Now, let's everyone

Pat, realizing things are close to getting out of hand, decides to mediate between Bob and Burt slow down a minute. Shouting, accusing, and table thumping aren't going to get us anywhere. Now, Bob, your subcommittee appears to have a number of concerns about detention. Right?

and ignore the off-topic issues that Thurmond introduced. First she tries a little humor, likening the disagreement to an athletic contest. Next she appeals to heretofore unspoken norms of courtesy in communication. Then she tries to make sure that the issues will be clarified to everyone's satisfaction.

BOB: You bet. We've got a report that lists 22—

He is still hot but slowing down.

PAT: OK. OK. Now Burt, here, thinks there may be explanations that justify what they're doing, given their limited resources, right?

BURT: Definitely.

Note her use of Summarizing here to show both Bob and Burt that she has been listening, yet is not on either side.

PAT: Well, let's just remember why we're here. One of the things the judge hoped we could do is help locate things that the court needs, like a new pool table and more recreation equipment in general. And no one said things at the court were perfect. Not the Judge. Nobody. Our job is to try and help, and to speak for the community about the way we'd like to see the court run.

That's a big job and it's going to take time. And it's not going to get done if we choose sides and treat these meetings like a football scrimmage. I get all of that I need at home from my big 17-year-old fullback! So, Bob, can we take these one at a time, slowly, without the fireworks?

Now Pat reminds them of the committee's overall purpose and of the problems they jointly face, as well as their contract (we can only guess at this but the eventual acquiescence of Bob suggests the contract was negotiated) to work cooperatively on finding solutions to the court's problems.

Again Pat uses a bit of homespun humor to ease the situation.

BOB: Yeah, sure, Pat. Look I'm sorry. But I've got it off my chest now. So—OK. Let's start with the physical plant—like those showers.

BURT: Great. Because if this group can get the hot water flowing again, it'll be a miracle.

Burt grabs the shower issue—clearly he's just as troubled by this as is Bob. There will continue to be differences between them, but for the moment they can work together harmoniously.

WILLIAM: Well, you know the motto of the Seabees: "The difficult we do immediately; the impossible takes a little longer."

William, the peacemaker, offers the group an uplifting motto.

PHIL: Will, your Korean War grey hairs are showing!

Phil, perhaps relieved that the fight is over, gets into the spirit of things.

No doubt there will continue to be sharp disagreements within the group, but in the future, members may consider how best to present their concerns, without necessarily seeming to attack the court's staff members who are present.

EXERCISE

Goal

When participating in a group, you should be able to recognize when Mediating is needed and be able to Mediate disagreements in a way that leads to their resolution.

Time Required

Depends on the time available—save about 20 minutes after the exercise for discussion of separate role plays by the entire group.

Materials

The role play instructions; separate copies of the several roles (i.e., cut up in such a way that each player gets only a copy of his or her own role description). Both A and B (or C and D), however, would each receive a copy of the short script that is used to start the role play.

Specialized Roles

Subgroups of four should be created, with a Mediator, an Observer, and two Role Players. If your group consists of an odd number of members, you could create two groups, with one subgroup having two Observers. If time allows, you may want to rotate the roles, so that each participant has a chance to play the Mediator role. The Observer's role is one of nonparticipation in the role play, followed by feedback to the Mediator in the discussion following each role play (for example, after the A/B role play). Incidentally, feel free to vary the gender of the persons being role played, depending on the composition of each subgroup; for example, "Bob" could just as easily be "Barbara." You may also decide to vary other descriptive attributes of the role players, depending on your group's composition.

Process

After you break into subgroups, begin the procedure that will guide each subgroup into a role-playing exercise. After each subgroup is formed and the roles of A, B, Mediator, and Observer(s) have been assigned, ask members not to read the instructions for any part other than their own. Also, ask them to ignore all of the instructions for the second role play (C and D). Next, perform the role play, having subgroup members switch positions only if time allows. As it is not possible to predict the amount of time you will have left at this point (that is, before doing the role plays) I suggest that you decide to allot some time—say, 20 minutes—for reassembling the total group so as to share your experiences, with reference to the write-up on Mediating. To begin the role play, A and B (or C and D) read from the short "starting" script. The Mediator is then free to mediate whenever and however he or she sees fit. The role play continues until the conflict situation is resolved or appears to be unresolvable; at either point, stop the role play and review the process, with reference to the write-up on Mediating.

FIRST ROLE PLAY (A AND B)

Mediator's Role

You are an employment counselor working with a group that is designed to help young adults prepare for job training programs. Arthur

Williams, a young black man, is heading for a food handler's course. He is sensitive about his race. You have sensed that there is tension between Arthur and Bob Smith, who is white and does not like black people. Bob is a veteran who had been a medic in the Army. He is planning to enter a training program for inhalation therapists. During a group meeting, Arthur and Bob get into an argument.

SECOND ROLE PLAY (C AND D)

Mediator's Role

You are the floor supervisor for Carla Brown and Dolores Lopez, two aides who work on the same floor of the hospital. Carla has been at the hospital for 2 years, does good work, and is going to school part time to become a hospital administrator. Dolores is in a training program for aides. She is young and careless with hospital procedures and routines, but well liked by most staff and patients. You are aware of the growing antagonism between Carla and Dolores. You discover them arguing when they should be caring for a patient.

SCRIPTS FOR MEDIATING EXERCISE FOR A AND C ROLES

Arthur William's (A) Role

You are a member of a group that is designed to prepare people (who need jobs) for job training programs. You are 19, black, and proud of being black. In your opinion, most white people are out to put you down; you suspect this is certainly true of Bob Smith (B). So far, you have avoided an open conflict with Bob because you want to get through this group without any trouble. You see the group as one of the things you have to do to get into a training program, but Bob continually irritates you. You dropped out of high school to support your mother and three younger sisters after your father died. Since that time, you have drifted from one job to another, but never found anything with a solid future. After a while you became depressed and began to play around with drugs. This led to an arrest and near conviction. This incident caused you to decide that you had better find a stable career. You have always liked cooking and are scheduled to enter a food handler's course shortly. At this point, the group is discussing problems related to arriving on time at work.

SCRIPT 1

A: Yeah, well you can say what you like, but I think a man shouldn't have to be split-second on time every day if he does the job well.

B: Say, who do you think will hire you with that attitude?

A: What do you mean? I said you gotta do the job right. A few minutes one way or the other—

B: [Interrupts.] Yeah, well, you can't even get it together enough to get here on time. We're always having to wait for you before we start meetings.

A: [Make it up from here. . .]

Carla Brown's (C) Role

This scene takes place in a hospital. You are a regular member of the hospital's staff, in your early 30s. You have been an aide for 2 years and have received two merit pay increases during that time. You have a family at home and are attempting to improve your earning potential by pursuing a degree in hospital administration part time at a local university. Prior to beginning work in the hospital, you held a number of sales positions; none of these was particularly interesting, but they provided a living. You have enjoyed your job in the hospital and see it as a first step toward a career in hospital administration.

In your opinion, Dolores (D), who is a trainee, is a loudmouth who works hard whenever a supervisor is watching, but tends to be irresponsible about hospital rules and procedures. Dolores often leaves the jobs she should do for others to do. She is disrespectful to you in spite of the differences in your ages, and she is unwilling to cooperate with you on any tasks unless specifically ordered to do so by your supervisor.

At this point, you have discovered Dolores taking a cigarette break in a place where smoking is forbidden. She was supposed to join you 15 minutes ago to help move a patient back to her room following surgery. Your initial approach is intended to be tactful, cheerful, but firm about the job to be done.

SCRIPT 2

C: How ya doin'?

D: OK, but my feet are killing me.

C: You'll get used to it. Ready to move the patient back to her room?

D: What patient? No one said anything to me about moving any patient.

C: [Make it up from here. . .]

SCRIPTS FOR MEDIATING EXERCISE FOR B AND D ROLES

Bob Smith's (B) Role

You are a 31- year-old Army veteran who dropped out of school and joined the Army because you thought school was not getting you anywhere. While in the service, you completed work on your diploma and received the general education degree. In the Army, you had a friend who was a medic, and when you could go into a training program for inhalation therapists, you jumped at the chance.

You do not like Arthur Williams (A). Arthur is black, and you have always been uncomfortable with black people. You had several fights with blacks who were fellow students in high school, and you never made any friends among black students. Arthur also irritates you because he always comes late to the group's meetings. He strikes you as a mess-up who always tries to work the easiest deal for himself and is really lazy.

SCRIPT 1

A: Yeah, well, you can say what you like, but I think a man shouldn't have to be split-second on time every day if he does the job well.

B: Say, who do you think will hire you with that attitude?

A: What do you mean? I said you gotta do the job right. A few minutes one way or the other—

B: [Interrupts.] Yeah, well you can't even get it together enough to get here on time. We're always having to wait for you before we start the meetings.

A: [Make it up from here. . .]

Dolores Lopez's (D) Role

This scene takes place in a hospital that has a training program for aides. You are 19 years old and a participant in a training program in the hospital. You have found your job to be dull and routine, but at least you are making some money and can see that you will make a steady income in the future. You have found yourself to be more interested in the different kinds of people you have met in the hospital than in your caretaking duties. You have become aware of several well-paid technician positions in medicine and think you would like to pursue this when you finish your current training program.

You view Carla Brown (C) as unfriendly, officious, and always looking to find fault with your work. No matter how hard you work, she always swoops down on you from nowhere when you are taking a rest between chores. As this scene begins, Carla has caught you having a cigarette break after you just finished putting an enormous load of supplies and linens away, something she could not know. She has made it clear that she does not like you and you have had just about all of the trouble from her that you want.

SCRIPT 2

C: How ya doin'?

D: OK, but my feet are killing me.

C: You'll get used to it. Ready to move the patient back to her room?

D: What patient? No one said anything to me about moving any patient.

C: [Make it up from here. . .]

POSTSCRIPT: ISSUES IN MEDIATING

Many group leaders and group members avoid conflict like the plague because of the mistaken notion that a group in conflict is a group in trouble. Actually, conflict, defined as "a struggle over values and claims to scarce status, power and resources in which the aims of the opponents are to neutralize, injure or eliminate their rivals" (Coser, 1956, p. 8) is (a) inevitable in any human group, and (b) potentially constructive. In his book, *The Functions of Social Conflict*, Coser (1956) discusses conditions under which conflict, if dealt with effectively, can actually foster the development of human relationships.

First, he points to the ways in which conflicts *between* groups serve to "establish and maintain the identity and boundary lines of. . . groups" (Coser, 1956, p. 38). But our concern lies more *within* a single group. In this regard, he notes that conflict within a group at least creates a relationship that "eliminates the accumulation of blocked and hostile dispositions by allowing their free behavioral expression" (Coser, 1956, p. 39). In other words, in the long run (he says) it is better to express, and thus define the areas of conflict, than to suppress them. With the conflict openly expressed, the group can work on resolving it. The goal is a resolution that is at least acceptable to all. But unless the conflict is openly discussed, festering hostility can lead to blocked communication, a lessening of attraction to the group (with its negative impact on group cohesion), and eventual ineffectiveness as a group. Further, a conflict unresolved can lead members to actually withdraw from the group, which, in terms of our interests in this book, would not be considered a good outcome.

Second, Coser (1956) notes that the nearer the subject of the conflict is to some critical aspects of the group's purpose for being, the more intense it will be. Thus, for example, a conflict about a major group goal could be expected to be a more powerful conflict than one dealing with disagreements about how best to achieve that particular goal. However, the exposition of a conflict over a major group goal, although it can represent a critical challenge to the group's very existence, is potentially useful because its resolution can unify the group's members on a very central issue, making it possible to tolerate conflicts about "lesser" issues.

Third, sometimes conflict boils up when one member expresses a position that is in conflict with the rest of the group. Coser (1956) refers to such an individual as a "renegade" and notes that this conflict can help to unify the rest of the group in its defense of some important aspect of the group. Unfortunately, this can mean the loss of that member, at the same time that the group as a whole is strengthened, and this is occasionally a reality of group life.

Fourth and finally, in his discussion of conflict, Coser (1956) makes a comment that is relevant to our discussion of Mediating,

> The mediator's function is primarily to eliminate tension, which merely seeks release so that realistic contentions can be dealt with without interference. In addition, he may suggest various ways to conduct the conflict, pointing out the relative advantages and costs of each. . . The main function of the mediator is seen as divesting conflict situations of nonrealistic elements of aggressiveness so as to allow the contenders to deal realistically with the divergent claims at issue. (p. 59 ff.)

IN PREPARATION

The exercise for Starting involves the development of a plan for starting a real group to which someone belongs, preferably one in which he or she has formal leadership responsibility and therefore one in which he or she is likely to use *this* plan for starting *that* meeting. Therefore bring a plan for starting a meeting to the next meeting of *this* group.

NOTE

1. I have borrowed this term from the work of Redl and Wineman (1957) in their chapter on "Techniques for the Antiseptic Manipulation of Surface Behavior" (p. 414 f). It is well worth reading for anyone who is involved with individuals who display difficult behavior.

SUGGESTED READINGS

Banyan, C., & Antes, J. (1992). Therapeutic benefits of interest-based mediation. *Hospital and Community Psychiatry, 43*(7), 738-739.

Carnevale, P., & Pruitt, D. (1992). Negotiation and mediation. *Annual Review of Psychology, 43*, 531-582.

Fisher, R. (1980). A third-party consultation workshop on the India-Pakistan conflict. *Journal of Social Psychology, 112*(2), 191-206.

Higgins, A., & Priest. S. (1990). Resolving conflicts between young people. *Educational Psychology in Practice, 6*(2), 60-64.

Lawson, R. (1989). Family mediation: Ethical issues and practice standards. *Australian Journal of Sex, Marriage and Family, 10*(4), 180-194.

LeResche, D. (1992). Comparison of the American mediation process with Korean-American harmony restoration process. *Mediation Quarterly, 9*(4), 323-339.

Maxwell, D. (1992). Gender differences in mediation style and their impact on mediator effectiveness. *Mediation Quarterly, 9*(4), 353-364.

Umbreit, M. (1991). Mediation of youth conflict: A multi-system perspective. *Child and Adolescent Social Work Journal, 8*(2), 141-153.

Volpe, M., & Lindner, C. (1991). Mediation and probation: The presentence investigation. *Mediation Quarterly, 9*(1), 47-61.

Chapter 13

STARTING

HOW DO YOU DESCRIBE STARTING?

Starting is a set of behaviors used to begin a group meeting or to introduce a new topic. Starting is intended to get the members relaxed, interested, willing to work, and focused on the group's business.

What is an example of Starting that you have seen recently?

_____

_____

_____

WHEN SHOULD STARTING BE USED?

To Open the Meeting

Open a meeting at the agreed-upon time, or as soon as all but one or two of the members are present. However, a meeting actually starts when the first two people arrive. Thus you have to differentiate between the official and unofficial start of a meeting and use Starting behaviors in relation to both.

To Introduce a New Subject

Introduce a new subject when the group has come to a consensus about the problem it had been discussing, dealt with an item on its agenda (if it has an agenda), or agreed that the topic should be set aside until a later time and appears ready to move on to the next topic or to another member's issue. If your example of Starting deals with a topical shift, was it done at the right time? Why do you think so? (Skip this question if your example deals with Starting at the *beginning* of a meeting.)

HOW DO YOU KNOW THAT STARTING HAS BEEN DONE CORRECTLY?[1]

1. All participants will be seated or positioned in such a way as to make it possible for them to attend to one another comfortably.
2. Participants, with few or no exceptions, will terminate behaviors and/or conversations not relevant to the agenda.
3. Participants, with few or no exceptions, will recognize that the Starting behavior has merged into the group's work and will participate actively.
4. Participants who expressed confusion about group goals during pregroup individualized Contract Negotiations would, if asked, report considerably less confusion following the use of Starting behavior.

HOW SHOULD STARTING BE DONE?

First, ask yourself what you hope the group will look like 5 minutes after it begins, and why. For example, at the end of 5 minutes, you might want members to be Attending to one another, conversation that is irrelevant to group matters will have ceased, members will be showing by their behavior that they are interested in the activity of the group, one or more members will have raised questions that are relevant to the group's contract, members will have begun to work on the business that has brought the group together, and so on.

Second, ask yourself what opening statements and actions are likely to be recognized as relevant and which ones will be enjoyed, so that the start of the discussion is interesting and attractive. Starting should help the group develop a feeling of unity, an awareness of common purpose, a sense of direction, and an ease with each other. In short, you want to help them work together so that they feel that they *are* a group or are

172 GROUP PARTICIPATION

going to become one. The first few minutes of the meeting represent a key point in time; it sets the stage for whatever follows. The way in which the beginning of a meeting is structured can determine the complexity of interaction that follows, and the nature of relationships that develop. For example,

> individuals who came to a conference were asked (as the meeting began) to first fill out an attitude questionnaire that was to be used as the basis of the group's discussion. Unfortunately, the questionnaire took 15 minutes to complete—15 minutes of zero interaction. When the conference leaders attempted to elicit interaction (once the questionnaires were completed), they got little response. The conferees had gotten a message that interaction was not desired and were reluctant to say anything.

In the write-up that follows, a great many possibilities are offered: Pick the ones you like, rather than feel that you must use them all.

Before the Meeting Begins

The way in which a meeting place is set up before people arrive can strongly influence what happens once they arrive. Here are a few facts about group life:

Members rarely, if ever, arrive all at once. So ask yourself what you want them to experience when they do arrive while waiting for others.

In a first meeting, people are likely to be wary, because it is a new situation. Even if they are uncomfortable with what they experience upon entering—such as the arrangement of chairs—they are unlikely to try to change it, at first.

People who are new to a group will look for clues about how to behave from:

1. The physical set-up of chairs, an available coffee pot, visible equipment, or materials.
2. Your behavior: seated and reading versus standing, verbalizing a greeting and shaking hands, or introducing people to one another.
3. The behavior of other people present: isolated, cautious, helping to set up chairs and tables, reading handouts, smoking, and so on.
4. The absence of ash trays to signify no smoking. (In some buildings, signs are posted prohibiting smoking, so this may not be an issue.)

People will settle into a group that is new to them with greater comfort if they are given something to do with which they are familiar while waiting for everyone to arrive:

1. Help themselves to coffee.

    2. Select a chair.

    3. Fill out a short form.

    4. Respond to your friendly greeting with small talk.

    5. Read a handout or agenda that lists expectations for this meeting.

    6. Help you set up equipment (e.g., a newsprint pad that the group will be using in the meeting).

Leaders often have opening night jitters about starting a group. This is absolutely normal, so it helps if the Leader has something to do that is relevant to the group, such as greeting people and introducing them to one another.

All of the above suggest that group leaders prepare in the following ways:

1. Make sure there are enough chairs for everyone.

2. Place chairs in a circle (or around tables formed into a square) for smaller groups (3 to 15): This helps people talk to one another. Chairs should be set up when people arrive. Or as a means of getting things started, early arrivers could be asked to help set up the chairs. The room should look as if it is available and ready for this group. Some people prefer to do without tables because they act as buffers between people and may inhibit communication. Actually, this depends on the purpose of the group and on the degree of its development. Committees, for example, often need tables so that they can inspect documents on which they are working.

3. Provide easy access to refreshments, cups, and such.

4. Have materials available for making easily read name tags (e.g., thick black felt pens, white 5-x-8 cards to be folded lengthwise). Make sure that the name cards are readable at a distance of 6 to 8 feet.

5. Set up equipment, such as a tape recorder or a chalkboard, so that they are ready for use. (Nothing is more frustrating than finding no chalk in the ledge at the bottom of a chalkboard!)

6. Check to make sure that you have a comfortable room temperature, ventilation, lighting, and so on.

To summarize:

- Plan ahead!
- Arrive early!
- Involve early arrivers!
- Stay loose!

"Openers": Different Approaches to Starting a Group

Let us assume that the official starting time for a new group has been reached and that all but one or two members are present:[2]

Forthright statement

The leader gives a brief statement of the nature and purpose of the group, which includes the following:

1. The formal Leader's name (if there is a Leader) and his or her official position in this group.
2. Name of the group, if it has one, such as "Orientation Group."
3. Objectives for this session; that is, what the Leader hopes will be accomplished as a result of this meeting.
4. What is going to occur in this session and the initial plan for the order in which it will happen.
5. A check to see if anyone present wants to propose a change in the plan or agenda, and to deal with any such proposals (e.g., enlarge the agenda).
6. A "go-round" in which members identify themselves.

For example:

[The Leader's voice is raised to attract attention.] "OK, let's get started." [Pause until everyone is paying attention.] "My name is Perry Jones. I'm a counselor here, and I'll be working with this Job Clinic group. As you know, we'll meet for four sessions, three times this week and once next week, to help you learn more about getting a job. By the end of these sessions, we ought to know something about each other's job-finding experiences. We should have begun also to develop good ways of finding out where the jobs are and how to sell yourself to an employer. By Thursday, you'll each be ready to go out to a particular job site and apply for work. Before we get started, however, it would help to know what you expected the group to be like. Would someone get us started by saying what he or she expected from Job Clinic?" [Pause, count to 10—if no one volunteers, suggest:] "Maybe it would help if we went around the table. How about it, Jim?" [The attempt here is to elicit a discussion of expectations, both to uncover and correct any incorrect information, and to get people talking. After this, the Leader might want to say something like:] "OK. Now that we've started, I thought it would help if we got to know each other because each of you has probably found out some things from your own experience that could help others here. The reason we have groups like this is that we've found that people can help one another a lot; for example, we could let each other know the things we are doing that seem to work well or not so well. To do this we have to know each other, not just as names like those on your name tags—that helps, of course—but something about each other. So here's what I'd like you to do to get us started . . ."

Starting a Meeting

Try to keep these actions relevant to this group. If members are in the group because they have significant problems in social functioning, they may be tense and have no patience with "fun and games." A wide range of activities can be used to start a group. The ones we have chosen can be characterized as follows: (a) verbal, (b) action, (c) recognition, (d) encounter, and (e) laughers. An example of each follows (obviously there are many more: You'll find source books that include good "openers" listed in the suggested readings at the end of this chapter):

1. Verbal. To start people talking to one another, bring an index card for each member with information you already have, such as their address and place of birth—information you believe the members would be willing to share. Give one card to each person; make sure he or she does not get his or her own. Each member reads his or her card aloud and tries to guess which card belongs to which member by watching the reactions of others. If he or she guesses correctly, he or she can then ask that person one question about himself or herself that is relevant to this group.

Another verbal beginning could be to break the group into subgroups of two or three persons. Give each a copy of an attitude questionnaire (3 to 5 questions) concerning issues that are likely to be dealt with by this group. Ask them to complete the questionnaire individually in no more than 5 minutes. Then ask them to work toward a consensual position on each item. Allow 15 to 20 minutes for this discussion. Give them a 5-minute warning, then 1-minute, before you want them to stop. Ask each subgroup to report its position (even if agreement was not reached) to the larger group.

2. Action. To start people doing something together, cut out a fair-sized picture (and glue it to cardboard) of someone or something with which members are likely to be familiar, such as a photograph of someone they all know. Cut it into three times as many irregularly shaped pieces as there are members, like a jigsaw puzzle. Give each member three pieces. Ask the group to assemble the picture within a limited period of time. Raise questions about the various roles people took in the task—the leader, the approver, the skilled technician, the loner, the talker—and relate this to the need for working together in this group to achieve desired goals.

A good variant of this starter is to divide the group in half, provide *each* subgroup with 100 or so sheets of 8 ½" x 11" paper, and a stapler.

Within a limited time (e.g., 15 minutes) they are to see which team can build the tallest free-standing tower. First, give them a limited time (e.g., 10 minutes) to plan. This could include building some prototypes, but not actually to begin. At the end of the building time, award a prize for the tallest tower and then a consolation prize to the losing team just for participating (such as lollipops) then discuss the experience, as suggested in the previous paragraph.

3. Recognition. To get people talking, moving together, helping one another, pin the names of different famous persons (written on 3 x 5 cards) to each person's back as the members arrive. For example, if all members are from one ethnic group, you could select well-known persons from this ethnic group. Members circulate, asking each other questions about the person whose name is pinned to their back to guess the name of that person. Members can only answer one another's questions with "yes" or "no". At a given time, the members sit and each tries to guess the name of his or her person.

4. Encounter. This is used in relation to an established group contract (e.g., used to begin meetings other than the first one).

Based on one of the problems the group has agreed to work on, make up lists of open-ended sentences, pair members off (an easy way to do this is to pair neighbors as they are seated), give them copies of the lists, and let them complete the sentences to one another, discussing the outcomes. For example, assume that the group exists to help members develop job search skills. Open-ended sentence lists might look something like:

- My name is . . .
- The reason I'm here is . . .
- When I think about looking for a job, I . . .
- When I go for a job interview, I . . .
- The thing about a job that worries me most is . . .
- I'm happiest when . . .

After a previously agreed-upon time limit, the group is reconvened and members are asked to discuss the sentence that—for them—created the greatest difficulty or the most interest.

5. Laughers. This is used when group members have come to know one another and you want a way to begin a meeting that is different and likely to loosen people up.

This approach depends on your style. Some people are more comfortable getting down to business and using humor spontaneously during group meetings. One Leader began some meetings with mock dramatic readings of a weather report. Another started groups by having members sing a silly song, in a straightforward way, until everyone realized it was silly and began laughing. Using humor is not everyone's cup of tea, but it can be effective.

Introductions. Ask members to pair off where they sit and to interview each other for information that is relevant to this group. Allow 5 to 10 minutes, telling them first that they will be asked to introduce each other to the group at the end of the interviews. You might suggest that everyone learn certain basic facts about each other, depending on the nature of your group; for example, where they were born, favorite music, hobbies, prior work experience, and such. You might, depending on the purpose and composition, direct each inter-viewer to ask some off-the-wall question, such as, "What is your secret ambition?" This gives the interviewer a way to begin. (Avoid going around the group asking each person to identify him- or herself— this is usually not heard by all and certainly not retained by any but a memory expert.) Once members have been introduced by their partners, they could be asked to state their expectation of this group experience (assuming you have not already done this). This provides a point of reference for other participants who can refer to similarities or differ-ences in expectations and how they fit into the proposed purposes for this group. In addition, it is possible for other participants to comment on or ask for information on significant facts brought out during the introduction; for example, if a person has recently moved into the city, how does she or he like it, and so on. Participants should be encouraged to query one another; it gets them talking to each other (not just to the Leader).

Refreshments. To make people comfortable and welcome, have some-thing to eat or drink that is likely to appeal to the participants. Let them help themselves as they arrive. Refreshments are usually most effective when given at the *beginning* of a meeting, not at the end. In selecting refreshments, it helps to pay attention to good nutrition and to avoid high fat, high calorie items, such as glazed doughnuts: Possibilities include grapes, tangerine sections, and so on.

Writing. To ease people into sharing ideas about the group, ask people to write down one or more of their reasons for joining the group and then read (out loud) and discuss what they have written.

Common reading. To get people talking in a focused way on relevant but not immediately threatening material, prepare a one-page description of a "typical" member (similar to all of the individuals present, but not exactly like any of the members) and some problem he or she is confronting, similar to the problem they are facing or a problem that groups like this one typically face. Give each member a copy to read, with instructions to think about a solution to the fictitious problem. Talk about what the fictitious person or group should do regarding the problem as a lead-in to ways in which this group could help individual members with their concerns. Go on from there to real members and their real concerns.

Role play. In most groups, it is probably best to avoid the use of role play in a *first* meeting. Wait until people begin to feel more comfortable with one another before you ask them to participate in role playing.

To simulate a real situation, select a problem that is relevant to the group's purpose and ask for volunteers to enact specified roles as a way of focusing discussion on this problem. A good way to ease people into role playing is to have a prepared script for the actors (see Mediating) that sets the scene and gives them their first few lines, then leaves them to make it up from there. Another way to do this is to give them a brief written history of the character and then interview them about who they are (asking them to answer in their role) to get them warmed up for the part.[3]

These are only a few ways to start a group. I have not talked about the uses of field trips, inviting a speaker, showing a film, and so on, because these often involve special equipment or arrangements. There are many good resources in your public library that can be adapted to your purpose, including materials such as instruction booklets prepared by national youth groups, recreation leaders' handbooks, guides to the use of audiovisual materials, and handbooks for discussion leaders (see this chapter's suggested readings).

EXERCISE

Goals

You will be able to start a group meeting in a way that puts members at their ease, helps each person understand the nature and purpose of this meeting, and engages members in interactions that are appropriate to the purpose of this meeting.

Time Required

At least one hour.

Materials

Varies with the Starting plan used.

Specialized Roles

None

Process

Select one kind of group that a group member is planning to develop or join, or in which he or she is now working. Plan a way of Starting one meeting for that group. Assign roles of members of the group, then role play that Starting procedure. A good follow-up to this exercise would be for members to actually use the procedure in Starting a group meeting, then reconvene the group to report on their experiences.

NOTES

1. This topic would usually come *after* "How Do You Start?" That section is so long, we have put this section here to give you a sense of the goals of Starting.

2. If there are *only* two or three present, it may have to be acknowledged that this is a problem. Stall for a limited time (e.g., 15 minutes), and if no one shows by then, negotiate a solution to this problem with those present, such as proceeding with those present, setting a new time, deciding how to ensure attendance of others, and so on.

3. Finding volunteer role players is not always easy. To avoid the discomfort of silence when asking for volunteers, people should be approached individually before the meeting starts and asked if they will help out in a role play. If they say "no" in this private situation, it is best not to pressure them.

SUGGESTED READINGS

Boyd, N. L. (1945, 1973). *Handbook of recreational games*. New York: Dover.

Corey, G., Corey, M. S., Callanan, P. J., & Russell, J. M. (1982). *Group techniques*. Monterey, CA: Brooks/Cole.

Doyle, M., & Strauss, D. (1976). *The new interaction method: How to make meetings work*. Chicago, IL: Playboy Press.

Fluegelman, A. (Ed.). (1976). *The new games book*. Garden City, NY: Dolphin Books/Doubleday.

Johnson, D. W., & Johnson, F. P. (1975). *Joining together: Group theory and group skills*. Englewood Cliffs, NY: Prentice Hall.

Pfeiffer, J. W., & Jones, J. E. (1969). *A handbook of structured experiences for human relations training* (Vols. I-V). San Diego, CA: University Associates.

Chapter 14

EPILOGUE
"Different Strokes for Different Folks"

INTRODUCTION

This book began with a discussion of the many ways in which groups can be described and analyzed. This was followed by fairly straightforward descriptions of 12 identifiable techniques that can be used to make a group successful, both in terms of goal achievement and member satisfaction. Each description was followed by a discussion of oppression and each technique's relevance to that issue, an example, and one or more participatory exercises— all of which were designed to bring the descriptions to life for you. Some who have used this book have referred to these descriptions, examples, and exercises as "simplistic," by which they meant—I guess—that working in or with a group is much more complex than the write-ups of each technique suggested. If that is what they meant by "simplistic" they are, of course, correct. It is one thing, for example, to speak of Confrontation in the abstract, but quite another to make such a description pertinent to a particular group, in a particular setting, at a particular point in time. Groups vary in so many ways—size, composition, goals, history, stage of group development, level of group cohesion, environmental conditions, quality of leadership, to name but a few—that it may feel simplistic to attempt to relate the descriptions in this book to *your* particular group realities. In concluding this book, therefore, I will attempt to address these complexities by describing briefly *the types of group* with which readers are likely to be dealing. I have chosen "group type" because different types of groups, by definition, are characterized by a number of critical conditions, and our group participation techniques must interact effectively with these critical conditions if your work in or with the group is to be successful.

In describing this typology of groups, it will be clear that my identification with the profession of social work has affected my choice: The group types I will identify are all used by social workers. I have included five major categories:

1. Individual-Change Groups
2. Educational Groups
3. Task Groups
4. Residential Groups
5. Support Groups

Because this does not cover the full spectrum of groups in our society, I will also comment briefly on some other types of groups. Five group types and 12 group participation techniques suggest an enormous 60-cell grid (e.g., Individual-Change Groups and Attending, Seeking and Giving Information, etc., or Attending as it pertains to Individual-Change Groups, Educational Groups, etc.). Either way would require a very lengthy exposition, and I am already stretching the page limits set on volumes in this Human Services Guide. Suffice it to say that any and all of the techniques can and should be used with each of the group types. Perhaps one does not use Responding to Feelings in an Individual-Change Group in the same way, or for the same reasons, that one uses this technique in a Task Group, but ignoring feelings in a Task Group is dangerous business and can lead members to feel alienated, as well as having a desire to get done with this particular group experience as soon as possible. In distinguishing these types, you will quickly note that the boundaries that separate them are not that discrete (e.g., changing individuals is a goal of both treatment and educational groups, etc.). But there is sufficient difference, I think, to justify identifying groups with one or another type, or in a few cases, as a mix of types.

TYPES OF GROUPS

Individual-Change Groups

Social workers, psychiatrists, psychologists, guidance counselors, and so on, are among the many professionals who use groups for therapeutic gain. These groups are for individuals who have significant problems with their self-concept and/or in their social relationships. In this vein, social workers have developed a method called "social group work" that focuses on the enhancement of social functioning (see, for example, Garvin, 1987; Northen, 1988; Rose and Edelson, 1987). Yalom (1983), a psychiatrist, has provided an excellent description of a method called "group psychotherapy" (see also Shaffer & Galinsky, 1989, which presents summary views of a number of therapy group approaches; e.g., Psychodrama, T-Groups, etc.). Both social group work and group psychotherapy are often used in mental health settings. Both tend to limit the size of the group to nine or fewer, and both rely heavily on group discussion managed by a professionally trained leader or set of co-leaders, although social group workers have historically made use of a wide variety of program activities to engage the interests of members. These activities were seen as a "means" to facilitate therapeutic gain, rather than as "ends" in themselves. Thus, for example, the square dancing club for children with chronic intractable asthma (the example in the chapter on Attending) was *not* designed to train its members to become expert dancers, but rather to have them engage in a normal social activity (where, in the past, parental fears of an asthmatic attack had kept each child wrapped in the proverbial "cotton batting") so that each member could begin to think of him- or herself as a "person with asthma," rather than as an "asthmatic person." This group even had a group goal: to demonstrate what they had learned by performing several dances for the other children at the Home. But again, the performance was simply another way of enhancing their social skills as individuals. Group psychotherapists, on the other hand, make no use of group goals (such as carrying out some task as a group) other than the goal of creating a group environment of mutual support. In therapy groups, members often challenge one another to reexamine patterns of belief and behavior, which hopefully will lead to the development of new insights. These insights can then lead to changes in the ways that members manage their social relationships. Other examples of Individual-Change Groups in this book include the Therapy Group in the chapter on Gatekeeping, the Adolescent Treatment Center Group in the chapter on Contract Negotiation, and the Mother's Group in the chapter on Summarizing.

Educational Groups

Educational groups are often found in academic settings where students meet together to carry out group projects or to participate together in a class (see, for example, Barchers, 1990; Pauly, 1991). Although the goal here is also individual change, there is no assumption made (as it is in Individual-Change Groups) that students have problems in self-concept or social functioning; rather, it is assumed that there is a body of knowledge and skill to be acquired, and the group setting can be used to facilitate the learning process. Keep in mind that there are many classes in which interaction among students within the classroom is not used, and is even actively discouraged, but it is hard to think of such classes as "groups"—at least not in terms of the definition of the term *group* set forth at the beginning of this book.

A different kind of educational group is a group designed to familiarize clients or patients with information about the way a particular agency works, or about a particular illness they (or a family member) have. For example, one-shot orientation groups are often used to introduce new patients and/or family members to a particular hospital service. Unlike the class group, membership consists of whoever shows up (often unpredictable) and, by design, participants do not return for a second meeting. Nevertheless, a considerable amount of critical information is made available, and members often interact in very meaningful ways (see, for example, Child & Getzel, 1989; Galinsky & Schopler, 1985; Phillips & Mankowski, 1991). Although several of the group scripts used as examples in different chapters included educational components, the one group that actually emphasized educational content was the Job Club in the Seeking and Giving Information chapter.

Task Groups

A prominent feature of a task group that differentiates it from the two types just described is its emphasis on the achievement of group goals. Examples of task groups include committees, boards, staff meetings, social action planning units, and athletic teams. All of these have one or more group tasks to accomplish, involving a process of problem identification and assessment, review of alternative strategies, decision making, implementation of a chosen strategy, and the evaluation of effectiveness (see, for example, Schindler-Rainman & Lippitt, with Cole, 1977; Seaman, 1981; Tropman, 1985). Task groups usually have formal leaders who may be appointed or elected to their position of leadership. Further, they are often guided by a set of written rules, such as bylaws.

Task group members are often members for a fairly long, predetermined period of time. They may represent themselves or some larger constituency. Group size varies widely, depending on the complexity of the tasks to be addressed and the history of the group. Although members will often want to change one another's points of view, "individual change" (of the treatment or therapy group variety) is definitely not a goal of a task group. Examples of task groups in this book include the PTO Committee in the Rewarding chapter, the Staff Meeting in the Focusing chapter, and the Citizens Advisory Committee in the chapter on Mediating.

Residential Groups

For some, institutional care is a required aspect of the community's response to their behavior—behavior that has often been of an antisocial nature. People in residential care are often involuntary members of a residential community (e.g., prison or psychiatric in-patient facility). Within the residential setting, a variety of groups can be found, including all of the other four types described here: therapy group, task groups (such as patient government), educational groups (designed to teach new skills for one's post-discharge existence), and support groups (see below). What makes the residential group different from all of the others is the 24-hour contact, or what Goffman (1962) calls the "total institution" (see also Trieschman, Whittaker, & Brendtro, 1969). In this country, large congregate institutions are gradually being fazed out (with the exception of prisons), partly because they are expensive to operate and partly because they appear to separate individuals from society to such an extent that it is difficult to achieve a satisfactory reintegration of residents back into the community following discharge. This has helped to create a large population of homeless individuals who now fit nowhere. Instead of large congregate institutions, many communities have come to rely on small group homes, which retain the benefits of group living in an around-the-clock protective and nurturing environment. Because these facilities are located *in* the community, residents can make regular use of local resources, outside of the group home (see, for example, Redl and Wineman, 1957), thus making it more natural to move back into full-time community living. Examples of residential groups in this book were the Promenaders in the Attending chapter, and Cottage Five in the Modeling chapter.

Support Groups

Alcoholics Anonymous was created by addicted persons because the community's social agencies had given up on providing service to them (Kurst, 1988). By design, these programs had no professional leadership. Early members created a 12-step problem-solving framework that they followed in helping one another "stay dry." In time, many support groups formed that were focused on problems other than alcohol abuse; some professionally led, some not, some using their own version of the 12-step framework (Gorski, 1991) while others relied on their professional leaders to provide direction to the group. Support groups are designed for people who share the same problem (e.g., survivors of child abuse), who have the same illness (e.g., multiple sclerosis), or are the "significant others" who live with and provide care for such individuals (see, for example, Nichols, 1991). (I was recently told that one difference between support groups and therapy groups is that support group members do not pay for their membership, whereas therapy group members do!) Examples of support groups in this book include the New Horizons Club in the Responding to Feeling chapter, and the Job Club in the Seeking and Giving Information chapter. (The latter is an example of a mix of the Education Group and Support Group, because it also taught particular social skills for managing interview and job-related work situations.)

There are, of course, other types of groups; for example, recreation groups, such as a square dance club whose purpose *is* to simply have fun and learn new dances; informal groups, small in membership, who happen to sit together in a classroom, then later, eat lunch together; and family groups, about which dozens of books could easily be (and indeed, already have been) written. The most comprehensive I have found is Goldenberg and Goldenberg (1985), which describes and compares six major approaches to family therapy in an even-handed fashion. The street gang group, used as an example in the chapter on Confrontation, is a kind of group that is not often found today. It seemed a good way to exemplify the use of Confrontation, and is known to me because, in fact, I was "Hank," and this was a group I worked with many years ago. In fact, most of the groups used as examples in this book were groups I worked with before entering academia. It was my experience that the so-called "detached worker" group-work approach used with street gangs—that is, detached from a building-centered program—never achieved widespread acceptance.[1]

IN CONCLUSION

In closing, let me share with you a talking blues I put together about treatment-focused group work to spur you on your way. And good luck with your groups, whichever type they are!

THE GROUP WORKER'S TALKING BLUES

(Note: Designed to be spoken rhythmically, while accompanied by hand-clapping at the bolded syllables or words.)

Now, if you **want** to help your **cli**-ents let me **tell** you what to **do.**
Just **put** 'em in a **group** with a **mem**-ber or **two.**
Get you a **room** with some **fair**-sized **space,**
Chairs and ta-bles, a **pri**-vate **place**—

You'll want interaction-interaction, group discussion-group discussion, high attendance-high attendance—something that will look good for the accountability buffs!

Now it **ain't** quite that **sim**-ple so I **bet**-ter ex-**plain,**
Just why you **want** to put your **cli**-ents on a **group** work **train,**
'Cause if you **bet** all your **mar**-bles on a **one**-on-**one,**
You **may** not reach your **goals,** and you **won't** have any **fun!**

You'll be sitting there . . . talking to yourself . . . listening to yourself . . . a real bore . . .

Say you **want** to start a **group,** but there's **none** where you **work,**
How do you **start** one without **look**-in' like a **jerk?**
Why not **pick** out a **prob**-lem that's **com**-mon to **man**-y,
Some-thing that's a **pain** for **John,** Jack, or **Jen**-ny.

Something psychological . . . sociological . . . biological . . . like, man, it really hurts!

You got a **group, now,** and you're **sit**-tin' **pret**-ty,
You can e-ven talk a-**bout** it to a **staff** com-**mit**-tee.
A **group** for **kids** who've been **kicked** out of **schools,**
The **kinds** of **kids** who've **bro**-ken all the **rules.**

Norm-busters . . . Limit-testers . . . Trouble-makers . . . The kinds of kids that are "emotionally disturbing!"

Say these **mem**-bers are be-**hav**-ing in a **way** that's out-**rag**-eous,
And it **runs** through the **group** til it's **quite** con-**tag**-ious.
You **try** to set some **lim**-its but the **mem**-bers will **yell,**
'Before we **do** what you **want,** we'll see you **roast** in **hell!'**
Well, they're **stand**-ing a-**round, feel**-ing mighty **slick,**
'Cause they **think** they've **got** their **wor**-ker **licked!**

When they **turn** a-**round**, and **what** do they **see**,
But a **calm**, cool **Wor**-ker, just a-**pass**-ing out **tea**!

And cookies . . . on doilies . . . that they all decorated in their last arts-and-crafts activity!

Now **friends**, you've **come** to the **har**-dest **time**,
The **mem**-bers will en-**deav**-or to **blow** away your **mind**.
They'll **push** you to the **lim**-it with a **test**-test-**test**.
For-cing a re-**sponse** that had **bet**-ter be your **best**!

Can you do it? Are you up to the challenge? Or are you just a quivering bowl of jelly?

Well, **if** you've read **Gar**-vin, **here's** what you'll **find**,
And **if** you've read **Nor**-then, **here's** what you'll **find**,
And **if** you've read **Rose**, **here's** what you'll **find**,
Or if you've **e**-ven read **Bert**-cher, **here's** what you'll **find**,
That if you **don't** let the **test**-ing **get** you **down**,
And **don't** de-**cide** that you're **going** to leave **town**,
But **help** the **group** achieve **self**-con-**trol**,
With **pos**-itive **growth** as their **num**-ber one **goal**,

You'll win! So what I mean is—take it easy, and take it!

NOTE

1. When I worked with such a group in Los Angeles in the early 1960s, there were a total of perhaps 10 professionals (4 of us working for a small Community Chest funded agency, and 6 in a unit of the County Probation Department) involved with between 20 and 30 gang groups. At that time, Los Angeles was reputed to have about 450 "fighting gangs" (see, for example, Klein, 1971).

REFERENCES

Bales, R. (1955). *Interaction process analysis: A method for the study of small groups.* Reading, MA: Addison-Wesley.

Bales, R. (1980). *SYMLOG case study kit.* New York: Free Press.

Bales, R., Cohen, S., & Williamson, S. (1979). *SYMLOG: A system for the multiple level observation of groups.* New York: Free Press.

Bales, R., & Strodbeck, F. (1951). Phases in group problem-solving. *Journal of Abnormal and Social Psychology, 46,* 485-495.

Barchers, S. (1990). *Creating and managing the literate classroom.* Englewood, CO: Teachers Idea Press.

Bertcher, H., & Maple, F. (1977). *Creating groups.* Beverly Hills, CA: Sage.

Block, L. (1985). On the potentiality and limits of time: The single-session group and the cancer patient. *Social Work With Groups, 8*(2), 81-100.

Cartwright, D., & Zander, A. (Eds.). (1968). *Group dynamics: Research and theory* (3rd ed.). New York: Harper & Row.

Coser, L. (1956). *Continuities in the study of social conflict.* New York: Free Press.

Child, R., & Getzel, G. (1989). Group work with inner city persons with AIDS. *Social Work With Groups, 12*(4), 65-80.

Fairweather, G. (1980). *Fairweather Lodge, a twenty-five year retrospective.* San Francisco, CA: Jossey-Bass.

Festinger, L. (1957). *A theory of cognitive dissonance.* Evanston, IL: Row, Peterson.

Festinger, L. & Aronson, E. (1969). Arousal and reduction of dissonance in social contexts. In D. Cartwright & A. Zander (Eds.), *Group Dynamics: Research and Theory,* (3rd ed.). New York: Harper & Row.

Foa, U. G. (1957). Relation of worker's expectation to satisfaction with supervisor. *Personnel Psychology, 10,* 161-168.

Forsyth, D. (1990). *Group dynamics* (2nd ed.). Pacific Grove, CA: Brooks/Cole.

Galinsky, M., & Schopler, J. (1985). Patterns of entry and exit in open-ended groups. *Social Work With Groups, 8,* 67-80.

Galinsky, M., & Schopler, J. (1989). Development patterns in open-ended groups. *Social Work With Groups, 12*(2), 99-114.

Garvin, C. (1987). *Contemporary group work* (2nd ed.). Englewood Cliffs, NJ: Prentice Hall.

Goffman, I. (1962). *Asylums: Essays on the social situations of mental patients and other inmates.* Chicago, IL: Aldine.

188

Goldenberg, I., & Goldenberg, H. (1985) *Family therapy: An overview* (2nd ed.). Monterey, CA: Brooks/Cole.

Gorski, T. (1991). *Understanding the twelve steps.* New York: Prentice Hall/Parkside.

Klein, M. (1971). *Street gangs and street workers.* Englewood Cliffs, NJ: Prentice Hall.

Kurst, E. (1988). *A. A. the story.* San Francisco, CA: Harper & Row.

Lewin, K., Lippitt, R., & White, R., (1939). Patterns of aggressive behaior in experimentally created "social climates." *Journal of Social Psychology, 10,* 271-299.

Losada, M., & Markovitch, S. (1990). Group analyzer: A system for dynamic analysis of group interaction. *Proceedings of the Twenty-Third Annual Hawaii International Conference on System Sciences* (pp. 101-110). (Copies *may* be available by writing to Marcial Losada, Ph.D., EDS Center for Machine Intelligence, 2001 Commonwealth Blvd., Ann Arbor, MI 48105.)

Milnes, J., & Bertcher, H. (1975). *Verbal empathic responding.* Ann Arbor, MI: Campus Publishers.

Nichols, K. (1991). *Leading a support group.* New York: Chapman & Hall.

Northen, H. (1955). The place of agency structure, philosophy, and policy in supporting group programs of social action programs. In H. Trecker (Ed.), *Group work foundations and frontiers* (pp. 236-247). New York: Whiteside & William Morrow.

Northen, H. (1988). *Social work with groups* (2nd ed.). New York: Columbia University Press.

Pauly, E. (1991). *The classroom crucible: What really works, what doesn't and why not.* New York: Basic Books.

Phillips, E., & Mankowski, M. (1991). Patient peer orientation groups: An innovative approach. *Perspectives in Psychiatric Care, 27*(2), 12-15.

Redl, F., & Wineman, D. (1957). *The aggressive child.* Glencoe, IL: Free Press.

Rose, S. (1989). *Working with adults in groups: Integrating cognitive-behavioral and small group strategies.* San Francisco: Jossey-Bass.

Rose, S., & Edelson, J. (1987). *Working with children and adolescents in groups.* San Francisco, CA: Jossey-Bass.

Schindler-Rainman, E., & Lippitt, R., with Cole, J. (1977). *Taking your meetings out of the doldrums.* La Jolla, CA: University Associates.

Seaman, D. (1981). *Working effectively with task-oriented groups.* New York: McGraw-Hill.

Shaffer, J., & Galinsky, M. D. (1989). *Models of group therapy* (2nd ed.). Englewood Cliffs, NJ: Prentice Hall.

Shaw, M. (1976). *Group dynamics: The psychology of small group behavior.* New York: McGraw-Hill.

Simmel, G. (1902). The number of members as determining the sociological form of the group. *American Journal of Sociology, 8,* 1-45, 158-196.

Solomon, A. (1992). Clinical diagnosis among diverse populations: A multicultural perspective. *Families in Society, 76*(6), 371-377.

Stogdill, R. M. (1974). *Handbook of leadership.* New York: Free Press.

Trieschman, A., Whittaker, J., & Brendtro, L. (1969). *The other 23 hours: Child-care work with emotionally disturbed children in a therapeutic milieu.* Chicago, IL: Aldine.

Tropman, J. (1985). *Meetings, how to make them work.* New York: Van Nostrand Reinhold.

Vroom, V. H., & Mann, F. C. (1960). Leader authoritarianism and employee attitudes. *Personnel Psychology, 13,* 125-140.

White, R. K., & Lippitt, R. (1960). *Autocracy and democracy.* New York: Harper & Row.

White, R. K., & Lippitt, R. (1968). Leader behavior and member reaction in three "social climates." In D. Cartwright & A. Zander (Eds.), *Group dynamics: Research and theory* (3rd ed., pp. 331-335). New York: Harper & Row.

World Book Dictionary, The. (1971). Chicago, IL: Doubleday.

Yalom, I. (1983). *Inpatient group psychotherapy.* New York: Basic Books.

The Answer to the Same-Same Dilemma

The key is in the unheard words of the first man. If he was a Truth-Teller he would say, "I am a Truth-Teller"; if he was a Liar he would lie and *say the same thing*, "I am a Truth-Teller." Therefore, we know that the second man gave an accurate report of what the first man said, which makes him—by definition—a Truth-Teller. Since #3 said #'s 1 and 2 were Liars, we now know #3 is a Liar. We also know that—because he lied about #2—he also lied about #1; therefore, #1 is also a Truth-Teller.

Incidentally, do not get hung up debating whether this is a fool-proof solution: After all, the focus is on Focusing, not any particular brain-teaser.

AUTHOR INDEX

SUBJECT INDEX

ABOUT THE AUTHOR

Harvey J. Bertcher is Professor of Social Work at the University of Michigan's School of Social Work. He has considerable experience in social work with groups, including work in residential and day treatment centers, street gang work, settlement houses and community centers, and group work with ex-psychiatric hospital patients and handicapped children. In recent years he has taken leadership in the development of group work by telephone, using conference-calling technology. He has served as consultant to human service agencies, including 3 years as the National Consultant in Social Work to the Office of the Surgeon General, the United States Air Force. He has coauthored several volumes, including *Creating Groups* (with Frank Maple) and *Role Modeling Role Playing* (with Jesse Gordon, et al.). He is also the author of *Staff Development in Human Service Organizations*.

#4404